787.1

A 1

Conversations with
MENUHIN

For Eva Seligman

Conversations
WITH
MENUHIN

Robin Daniels

Foreword by Lawrence Durrell

"The performer's rôle is to inspire the audience to follow him in his
devotion, his devotional act."
from the conversation on interpretation and performance

MACDONALD GENERAL BOOKS

Macdonald and Jane's · London and Sydney

Other books by Robin Daniels

BLACKPOOL FOOTBALL:
THE OFFICIAL CLUB HISTORY
(Robert Hale, 1972)

CONVERSATIONS WITH CARDUS
(Gollancz, 1976)

© Copyright 1979 by Robin Daniels and Zircon Anstalt

First published in Great Britain in 1979 by
Macdonald General Books
Macdonald and Jane's Publishers Ltd
Paulton House
8 Shepherdess Walk
London N1 7LW

ISBN 0 354 04428 1

Filmset in 12 on 13½ pt 'Monophoto' Sabon by
Servis Filmsetting Ltd, Manchester
Printed in Great Britain by
Purnell & Sons Ltd, Paulton (Bristol) and London

CONTENTS

ACKNOWLEDGEMENTS

I am most grateful to:

Lawrence Durrell, for writing the Foreword

Marie Mann and Ina Vincent, for expert typing and deciphering

Diana Menuhin and Kathleen Smith
also Caroline Taggart and Jock Curle for help with picture research

Yehudi Menuhin's secretary, Eleanor Hope, and the other members of his secretarial team, Fiona Eakins and Ruth Abel, for their prompt and cheerful help at all times

Alan Rowlands, my music teacher

The late Betty Mather and Peter Norris, member of staff at the Yehudi Menuhin School, for assistance with research

John Marsh and Joseph Ingram, for advice

Kauko Karjalainen, Executive Secretary of the Finnish Music Information Centre

The staff of the Buckingham Palace Road Library and Central Music Library, Westminster

The staff of the Royal Albert Hall and of the Goethe Institute, London

The author and publishers would like to thank the following for kind permission to reproduce the photographs used on the pages quoted:
Clive Barda – London: 52, 72, 149
Maria Bartha: 14, 123
Maurice Broomfield: 164
Camera Press: 120, 152 (photographs by Camilla Jessel)
Central Press Photos Ltd: 136
Decca Record Company Ltd: 92
David Farrell: 23, 49, 66, 68, 79, 105, 107, 133, 138, 167, 186
Foto Atelier Fäh Franz: 18, 21, 110–111
Fox Photos Ltd: 54–55
Godfrey Macdomnic (EMI Ltd): 156

Popperfoto: 160
Press Association/A.F.P.: 129
Report: 57 (photograph by Kurt Hutton)
The United Nations: 183 (photograph by Louis Falquet)
Gerd Volmer, Zurich Chamber Orchestra: 180
Penguin Books Ltd: 176 (photograph by Sandra Lousada)
Reg Wilson (EMI Ltd): 102

The photographs on pp. 39, 83 are by Erich Auerbach: p. 89 by Atelier E. Hoenisch of Leipzig; p. 171 by Hélène Jeanbrau; pp. 41, 97 by Ramon Scavelli; p. 86 by Jimmy Sileo of New York; p. 77 by the United States Armed Forces; p. 61 by Votovafoto of Vienna.

Any photograph, the source of which has not been traced, will be acknowledged in a future edition if the copyright holder has by then notified the publishers.

R.D.

FOREWORD
by Lawrence Durrell

THE DISTINCTIVE GIFT of Yehudi Menuhin has always seemed to me to reside in a perennial youthfulness. He is, so to speak, the Lark at Heaven's Gate.

Perhaps some of the gifts of his youth still inspire the adult life – so completely fulfilled and rounded – of one who transcended world success as a child and transformed the early acclaim into world success as an adult. His life is an extraordinary one: no novelist would dare invent such a story, for in real life the boy genius often fades as swiftly as he arrived.

In youth Menuhin was as sheltered as a seminarist. This enabled him to protect and perfect his gifts with unhurried deliberation. And even when, before adolescence, he had achieved world fame, he was able, thanks to the care of his mother and father, to sidestep the debauching effects of public triumph. His parents did not even show him his press cuttings!

But when he embarked on the sea of adulthood he found the journey difficult – for he lacked not only experience of people but also the teachings of struggle. Rough seas, in both art and personal life, threatened to defeat him. With passion and determination he managed to turn the tide and emerge once more among the top rank of virtuosi.

These relaxed and informal conversations with Robin Daniels give us a chance to meet Menuhin, not on the concert platform but in the privacy of his own home, in the workshop where he hammers out – or, more usually, discovers by intuition – his ideas and opinions.

This book portrays a singular soul, so daring, so ambitious and yet so modest. How refreshing that he has never lost his faith in the ability of mankind to save itself, to recover its lost birthright in the form of a just and humane world order.

Menuhin's eager pleading on behalf of man's nobler part puts to shame the tepid hearts and shrinking souls among us. Never has a busy public man responded to so many claims on his time or crammed his spare moments with such diverse activities.

His ardour burns in these conversations with an innocent sparkle and zeal.

Menuhin is as pious towards the concerns of his neighbour as he is towards his violin and his music scores. And yet, despite the uniqueness of his art, he never fails to nudge each one of us with a reminder that goodness, if practised enough, could become contagious.

Lawrence Durrell

INTRODUCTION

PLEASE COME WITH ME to the Albert Hall, not for a concert – not *this* time! – but to visit the basement and explore the archives room. High on a long, rickety shelf we find the volume we are looking for, a bound set of programmes from the winter of 1929–30. Coated with dust but in mint condition, probably unopened these last fifty years, the pages bring to momentary life an era which is both past and miraculously still present.

In quiet awe, we pause at each name. They are members of a musicians' Hall of Fame, not only of the last hundred years, but of all time: Rachmaninov, Ysaÿe, Kreisler, Tetrazzini, Chaliapin, Paul Robeson, the Cortot-Thibaud-Casals Trio; and on Sunday, 10 November 1929, the first London recital by a thirteen-year-old boy, Yehudi Menuhin. A week earlier, in the Queen's Hall, he had made his London *début*, playing the Brahms concerto with the London Symphony Orchestra under the baton of Fritz Busch. On the basis of a single performance, some of England's leading music critics were already speaking of Menuhin's genius.

His gifts were also recognized immediately by the foremost musicians of the day; a group jealous of its prestige, and notorious for prickliness towards a newcomer, they openly acknowledged his talent and welcomed him as one of their select number. To his fellow-musicians, Yehudi Menuhin was not a child prodigy; he was a violinist of the first rank who happened to be in his early teens. He was worthy of respect whatever his age. On the Menuhin mantelpiece are two autographed pictures from this period: one of Enesco, dedicated to 'My old young friend;' the other of Bruno Walter, inscribed 'To Yehudi Menuhin, the little boy with the great soul, from his friend for ever.'

With every passing year I become more aware of the subtle patterning which shapes all our encounters. In my meeting Yehudi Menuhin, this pattern was at work long before I was born. My mother lived in Forest Hills, New York, close to the Menuhin home when he was nine years old. Early in my childhood, she described how she used to see the young Yehudi, carrying his violin case. As my interest in music developed, I listened to Menuhin recordings and went to Menuhin concerts. One day I accompanied my music teacher, Alan Rowlands, to a lecture-recital at the Royal College of Music.

Keith Falkner said in his introduction that Menuhin was free to play the violin, talk, answer questions, and even, if he wished, stand on his head. Having done the first three, Menuhin beamed: 'And the last, standing on the head, that is the easiest.' He looked down at the floor as if to suggest the need of a mat. The Director spread his jacket on the platform. Menuhin, his back to the assembled students, knelt down. His legs rose to the vertical, slowly and with consummate control. He remained still. Then, by flexing one leg, he showed how a conductor could beat time for an orchestra while facing the audience upside down!

Visitors to Menuhin's school for young musicians instantly become aware of his character and influence. I remember one visit, on a day in summer; he wasn't there, but I felt his presence. My first impression was of laughter and spontaneity. As I walked along the path to the main entrance, I paused to watch some of the children playing cricket. At that moment there was an easy run-out, but the wicketkeeper delayed knocking down the stumps until the last possible second. This increased the excitement of the players – and of their audience of one. His masterstroke, finally and inevitably accomplished, won a burst of clapping from all the children – including the run-out batsman.

A few minutes later these children were in class or practice room, applying themselves to academic studies or their instrument with all the more freshness and vitality of heart and mind thanks to their moments of fun on the lawn. Not once did I detect an atmosphere of strain or élitism, or the pressures of a hothouse for intellectuals. On the contrary: I felt everywhere and with everyone the ease and informality of a large family.

Structured activities sometimes last from seven in the morning until seven at night, but the children thrive. Their exhaustion at the end of a long day is the tiredness of fulfilment, not the tiredness of frustration. The reason for this can be summed up in one word: balance.

Yehudi Menuhin's school is the epitome of balance: music alternating with academic studies; private practice followed by public performance; rest, storing energy for recreation; balance in diet; imagination and analytical skills given equal importance. Each day is dedicated to individual maturing and group harmony. Crucial also is the partnership between teacher and student. As Peter Norris, a piano teacher and the orchestra's conductor, says, 'This is a school and a setting in which the staff as well as the students can grow and develop.'

To Menuhin, balance is all-important: balance of mind and body, of giving and receiving, seriousness and humour, public life and private life, culture eastern and western. He has the wisdom of age and yet appears ageless. But don't be misled. Menuhin, idealist and visionary, is complemented by Menuhin the practical, who, if he were not a violinist, could have been a farmer, a doctor, or an inventor – or all three!

When Yehudi Menuhin and I met for the first time, we were already linked by our correspondence, our mutual friendship with Neville Cardus and my mother's glimpse of Menuhin all those years ago. Menuhin and I had both spent happy childhood days in San Francisco, that most liberal and liberating of cities, and now we were both starting a sabbatical. We met in his home at Highgate over a period of many months, allowing our book to evolve and emerge in its own time. The intuitive rapport between us is such that we agreed to work together on this book long before our first meeting.

Menuhin's public appearance, in evening dress on the concert platform, is known to thousands in every nation. How did he appear to me at our first encounter, in his own living room? I found little or no difference between his public self and private self. He is the most relaxed and most gracious of men; the gestures few; his humour drily ironic; the voice gentle and musical, distinctive in timbre, with its own individual rhythm and cadences. He selects words carefully but without affectation. Every emotion, every thought, every body movement, proceeds from a calm centre: Menuhin's presence is strong but not imposing. In a curious way, he seems larger of stature when seated than when standing. His profile is noble and aspiring, the answer to a sculptor's dream. Most revealing of all are the eyes: clear, benign, intuitive, far-seeing, ever active and yet motionless, searching deeply, inwardly and outwardly.

For over half a century Menuhin has given his life to the service of music. His fame spans continents as well as generations. The product of many rich cultures – Russian-Jewish parents; birthplace, New York; teachers from east and west Europe – he has become friend and citizen of all countries. He has touched the hearts and lives of men and women throughout the world, not only as musician but as advocate for freedom. He is an artist known and respected far beyond the boundaries of his art.

Home is where he and his family happen to be: India, Greece, California, Switzerland, Highgate. At all times of the day and night he receives phone calls from every part of the world with invitations to play, conduct, teach, and lecture. Menuhin is as much at home with the youngest violin student as with the most venerable of world statesmen. His range is enormous. He can speak with authority and imagination – and with no advance notice – about Bach and Bartók, architecture, Amnesty International, and the benefits of natural foods. Ideas flow from him like a stream of sparks.

He is a practitioner of what the wise Neville Cardus once said to me: 'Good conversation, like good writing, is discursive.' Menuhin casts new

Yehudi Menuhin relaxing with the author.

light on a hundred and one aspects of life – historical, artistic, metaphysical. His intuitive mind and his gift of free association lead him naturally from subject to subject.

Truly and widely he follows his own muse, accompanied and strengthened by his wife, Diana. He plays, conducts, teaches, records, organizes festivals, judges competitions, travels all over the world, lectures, writes, broadcasts, makes films, helps numerous charities and good causes on an international scale. He spends and spreads his energy prodigiously and generously. Despite this – perhaps because of it – he looks years younger than most men in their middle sixties. He is so much more than a musician; more even than music's world-wide ambassador. Menuhin is a rare and refined human being.

Genius, like the slanting rays of afternoon sunlight, casts a long shadow. Although daily discipline and practice are imperative, for the famous as well as for the lesser-known, the ultimate source of great performance, in music as in all art, is the experience of life *outside* the studio. Likewise, the most influential teacher is the one who has struggled hardest with his own technique and tone in those testing times, social as well as artistic, which creep up on every career, often when least expected, with the power to divert, crush, or goad forward.

All Menuhin's skill in violin playing, all his faculties of breadth of living and relating – I want these next words to be read as if underlined – have been hard-earned, and, at several fulcrum points in his life, were re-gained with difficulty, throb, and ache. The earlier the sun of genius rises, the darker the impending shadow may be.

What is this shadow which haunts genius? The forms it can take are many: some are open and combatable; others lie in wait, hidden, lurking, insidious. Every natural gift – whether of beauty or charm, or the ability to climb mountains, lead armies, or make money – every gift has a seductive quality: the danger is that the possessor will over-identify with his gift, and be over-identified with it in the eyes of other people.

If the gift falters or fails, a total crisis ensues; the whole personality is felt to be crumbling. What was accepted as a free gift and then lost, now has to be bought back by conscious and deliberate study of fundamentals. Indeed, the former owner of the gift may ask himself the most radical of questions: 'Do I *want* to buy it back? Am I willing to pay the price?' Perhaps for the first time in his life he has the choice of ownership.

The shadow may hover at other times and in other ways: in the need to throw off the burden of parental expectations, or in the hurtful realization that personal growth has not matched evolving creativity. A still-successful career may delay the impetus to resolve inner conflict, and can often precipitate problems in close relationships.

The shadow may appear at the time of retirement or in the form of an unrealistic attitude to the value and use of money . . . the catalogue of dangers would fill many volumes. Carl Jung rightly said: 'Great gifts are the fairest, and often the most dangerous, fruits on the tree of humanity. They hang on the weakest branches, which easily break.'

Attitude and awareness are *all*. Personal shadows usually *appear* as threats. If we can go beyond outward form and appearance, we shall see, and perhaps even welcome, these shadows for what they ultimately are – teachers of life. To Menuhin's enduring credit, and our lasting joy, he has confronted and learned from the dark side of his own rare gifts.

Menuhin has his critics; so does everybody who is known to a worldwide public. For myself, I yield to no one in my respect for Yehudi Menuhin, as man and as musician. His violin playing, at its best, has a giving, healing, life-enhancing quality: to listen is to participate; and in participation we are made more whole. To hear Menuhin play the G minor section of the first movement of the Beethoven concerto is one of the supreme musical and artistic experiences.

Menuhin on the concert platform does more than play the violin: he offers us a living re-creation of music, a spiritual search. For him, the most articulate of men, fluent in many languages, violin playing is an even more natural means of expression than the spoken word.

At a dinner recently, a German violinist was speaking with insight about the great instrumental players of the twentieth century. 'Menuhin for *Innigkeit*', he said, and then paused. In a spontaneous gesture, he bent his head above encircling arms, and added, '*Innig* is the word we use to describe the way a parent *cradles* a child.'

Robin Daniels

I

INFLUENCES

RD: The whole of the first section of the *Meditations* of Marcus Aurelius is devoted to thanking all those who had been an influence for good in his life: his mother and father, his grandparents, tutors, and friends. I wonder if you would now like to do the same?

YM: Yes, very much. To my wife, Diana, I owe the most; I also owe much to my parents and teachers, and certainly to my children. Even relationships with people I disliked have been very salutary for me.

Diana and I are in some respects quite similar; we are totally dedicated to the arts. Her training was in ballet; she knows a great deal of music, and was raised in a musical household. Gradually she has translated her specific knowledge and training into the wider art of life itself, an art in which I still make many faltering steps.

She has an intense longing for form, for perfect balance in whatever she does. Aesthetics are the basis of her *mores*. Through her influence and example, I have come to believe that aesthetics usually offer a good and workable guide, a more valid and flexible guide than moral *mores*, edicts, didactic catechisms.

Being so generous and so understanding of others, her aesthetics are not at all divorced from life. The touchstone of her *mores* is whether a thought, an action, a relationship, is aesthetic, harmonious, balanced.

This approach is not only pleasing to contemplate, it is highly practical in application. Take for example the morality – or lack of it – of a land and property speculator who builds cheap houses. If they are ugly, and ill-considered in design and in siting, they are bound to be less than humane. The speculator has given the minimum of time and thought to his project: he has not consulted the best architects or the best interior decorators; he has not spoken to housewives, to the type of people who might buy and live in these houses; he has not studied the needs of children, nor the relation between the housing estate and the community as a whole. This is ugliness of thought and action. His sole criterion has been money, the speed of return on investment. Even if such a person were to build dwellings that were more comfortable, they would be in the guise of what was opulent and prestigious. This would not in any way make the houses more beautiful.

Diana's sense of taste is unerringly assured, in dress, in voice, in emotion. Everything about her is aesthetically and morally pleasing. You will sometimes meet people whose manner and behaviour seem aesthetically pleasing but who have not established a rapport between aesthetics and morals. Once this rapport is established, life is transformed, and day-to-day living is guided by a perfectly sound compass: valid in your relationships

A Christmas gathering of the Menuhin family. (Left to right – standing: Gerard, Zamira, Krov, his wife Anne, Jeremy; seated: Diana, Yehudi, grandson Lin.

with children as well as with adults; valid in all decision-making, political, managerial, familial; valid with friends and with adversaries.

When I first saw Diana I realized she was the person I had been looking for all my life. She has devoted so much of herself to me and to my work; I hope she will yet have the time and opportunity to give free scope to her knowledge of prose and poetry, and to her enormous creative capacity. I wonder if you saw her two television programmes: one was based on the poetry of E. E. Cummings, and the other on Edward Lear. Diana recited from memory. The whole setting was almost operatic, with clothes, *décor*, and specially commissioned music, all chosen to match the mood and content of the poems. She has also taken part in performances of the *Carnival of Animals*, reciting her own verses, elegant, apt and witty.

In whatever she does, Diana behaves with absolute appropriateness. In the face of adversity, she acts with indomitable courage and valour. She is at her best in a crisis: the greater the pressure, the greater is her clarity and control. I always marvel at that, because I am the other way round. When I am really under pressure, I tend to lose my self-control. Perhaps that is why, all through my life, I have channelled my emotions and passions into music, and done everything possible to cultivate equanimity.

Diana, on the other hand, has such potential that she is at her best when geared to a seemingly impossible task, like a racing car which *relaxes* into a speed of 150 miles an hour and complains when it is doing less: it feels frustrated when its full power is not being used, and purrs quietly and contentedly as soon as it reaches the speed for which it was designed.

Whereas I try to reserve my energies – for a concert or a lecture – she cannot do that. She spends all her waking hours doing something, improving something: whatever I write, I submit to her, and inevitably it comes back transformed. Diana gives extravagantly of herself – in energy, dedication, and strength of will – for the good of others. I doubt if she knows the meaning of self-protection. She is an extraordinary wife and an extraordinary mother, having had to divide her life between my travelling and looking after our children. I couldn't possibly owe anybody else more than I owe her.

I have been incredibly fortunate all through my life in knowing so many *dedicated* people. Nobody could have had more utterly dedicated parents: if I can cavil at all, I would say that they were perhaps *too* dedicated. They did everything possible for me and for my sisters.

My mother and father protected me from publicity and the curiosity of the press: for a long time I never met a reporter and never read reviews of my concerts – and that was good for me. Family life was maintained despite my many concerts. We never spoke about money. We never touched on subjects that would deflect our sense of direction. Our life revolved around music, family, and friends.

My father kept me informed about important events, national and international. He used to cut out newspaper articles for me to read, and to this day he still sends me clippings which he thinks will be of interest.

My mother's main influence came from her knowledge of languages and literature. And of course we had some fine tutors. Hephzibah, Yaltah and I, were always surrounded by people who were *utterly* dedicated to their special subject, to their work, and to us.

As I look back, I can see that my first marriage was a kind of rebellion against being surrounded by people who were so dedicated. My choice fell upon a person who was lighthearted and exuberant, with hardly a care in the world and no great weight of purpose in life. Inevitably, our relationship broke down. Apart from that almost deliberate disintegration of a given life-style, I have been surrounded from my first waking moment by people of like mind and singleness of purpose: my parents, with their *complete* devotion to all three children; my three great teachers, Enesco, Persinger and Adolf Busch; Diana; and my many loyal friends and colleagues in the musical world, in every continent.

I shall always remember with gratitude Enesco's influence: his reverence for music, for all human beings, and for life itself; his chivalry towards women; and his almost ritualistic gentleness when speaking to a child. Whoever he was with, child or adult, famous or unknown, he always showed respect. There was enormous *style* in everything he was and did. Enesco was a wonderfully handsome man, with a mass of black hair, fine posture, and a commanding, romantic presence. In his music-making – whether with the violin or at the piano, whether conducting or singing, or just talking about music – Enesco was *igniting*. Busch didn't have the incandescence of Enesco, but nonetheless he was in the best German tradition of teachers and, like Enesco, had the utmost reverence for music.

Until you put your opening question to me, I had never before realized how continuously fortunate I have been in the people I have met and worked with. To this day, I am surrounded by people who share the same attitude to

Opposite: Yehudi and Hephzibah.

life, who serve to the best of their ability, and want to create the best possible atmosphere for the benefit of all. People without this attitude have dropped out of my life.

Here at home I have an excellent secretary, Eleanor Hope, who is extremely able and sweet-natured. She is a clear-thinking person and always willing to help. Anyone who visits my school [at Stoke d'Abernon in Surrey] will find an extension of this same atmosphere. This is not my doing; it is thanks to our charming headmaster, Peter Renshaw, and his wife, Virginia; and, before they came, Antony Brackenbury; and the staff, and the children themselves.

At the school we are trying to build a community on a foundation of wholeness, uniting the musical life, spiritual search, intellectual attainment, a sense of giving and sharing and mutual understanding, and a broad view of life, social, artistic, scientific, philosophical.

Perhaps this constant strand in my life – of dedication and of dedicated people – owes something to my father's rabbinical ancestors. My work, and the work of those around me, is not dedicated to victory *over* anyone; but if there is going to be a fight, I side with Polonius when he told Laertes, who was about to return to France:

> . . . *Beware*
> *Of entrance to a quarrel, but being in,*
> *Bear't that the opposed may beware of thee.*

I believe there can be much danger of cruelty and pain in a fight that isn't clearly concluded.

RD: In what ways have you been influenced by your children?

YM: Children keep adults young. They know their parents better than anyone else does, and are not usually inhibited in expressing criticism.

Our children are absolutely honest and reliable. They haven't taken to drink or drugs. They conduct their lives with integrity. They work hard and are financially solvent.

Children proceed in two directions: in part they follow and imitate, and in part they go in diametrically the opposite direction from their parents – this is an essential stage of growth. Who are they to test themselves against, even rebel against, if not their parents? And so there are periods of dissension and

Father and son, Yehudi and Jeremy.

readjustment, as children test you as parents, test your principles, test your whole way of life against what they find elsewhere. Having asserted their independence, and having proved to themselves that their parents were after all not far off the mark, children usually come back.

Diana has been scrupulous, never going into a child's room without knocking, never prying into secrets, never asking for information that wasn't voluntarily given. It is natural for a child to want to establish his autonomy, make his own decisions, learn from his own mistakes.

Our children keep us young and alert; without them, our way of life might veer towards pre-determined paths. We establish our routine, organize our concerts and our travels; but we need our children to keep us abreast of the times, to remind us of who we are, with our strengths and weaknesses, our oscillating between tension and relaxation. For pulling away the cobwebs of self-delusion, children are absolutely invaluable.

RD: To what extent were you inspired, in your boyhood, by the violinists who were then at their peak?

YM: Tremendously so. My idols were Heifetz and Kreisler. I also admired Mischa Elman for his unashamedly violinistic abandon. Like an Italian tenor who is seduced by the sound of his own voice, Elman was carried away by the temptations of the violin. He took sensual delight in making his instrument give forth some of the most gorgeous sounds ever heard. He had an extraordinary command and range of tone.

I admired Heifetz for his truly exceptional self-discipline and precision. His tone had a sort of high metallic sheen and gloss. Kreisler I adored for his tenderness, for the elusive enchantment of his playing, for transporting me to regions of elegance and romantic feeling which I hadn't yet known at first hand. I was a child. I knew so much, I felt so many emotions, but had never made their acquaintance! I felt the tragedy in life, I felt abandon, exuberance, exaltation, but hadn't met these feelings in the *outer* world.

My parents brought tenderness and joy, and concern for mankind, but in an enclosing, centripetal way, like the nurturing of a flower still in bud. Eventually, all these same emotions, which had been known only within the family circle, have to be looked for, rediscovered, from one's own initiative: no longer accepting feelings and experiences as coming to you from a circle concentrated on its centre – for I was the centre of my parents' life – but expressing them in one's own growing relationship with the outside world.

Opposite: 'Kreisler's playing was infinitely precious to me.'

This stage in life is a total turning inside-out of all that has been known in one realm only. What was centripetal becomes centrifugal, flows out from the centre. The bud bursts into bloom.

Kreisler's playing was infinitely precious to me. It told me of everything that was still to come: of Vienna, of cities I had never visited, of courtships as yet unknown. My greatest desire as a child was to play the violin as well as Heifetz and to *communicate* as Kreisler did.

When I was nine or ten, I played the *Dance of the Goblins*, Paganini's *Moto Perpetuo*, and the *Symphonie espagnole* of Lalo. Music critics who have listened to those recordings from my earliest years say that they stand comparison with Heifetz – I don't know why or how. But at that time it would have been *far* beyond me to have given the right inflection to the simplest notes of Kreisler's *Liebeslied* or *Liebesfreud* or *Schön Rosmarin*.

When I was about twenty, and had returned to Paris with my family, I was asked to record some of these Kreisler pieces. I thought to myself, 'This is my moment. I must now be able to play them.' I bought a record of Kreisler playing *Schön Rosmarin* and the *Caprice viennois*. I listened carefully and then did my best to emulate Kreisler. About two weeks later I made the recording and felt reasonably satisfied with it. In later years I played these Kreisler pieces a great deal; during the war, almost every day.

Heifetz I admired for his high degree of control and discipline. He could play with warmth, but the warmth was calculated with the precision of a computer. He knew exactly what he wanted, and there wasn't a note or a length or an accent or a *portamento* or *vibrato* that was not controlled; but he played – as someone with great self-discipline can – with a *seemingly* natural and effortless command.

The fact that Heifetz could produce each time the replica of previous performances is an amazing achievement, an example of supreme control. It was like being always on top form, and his top form included all the musical elements.

I don't think Heifetz left anything to chance. Every single note he played – by virtue of that sheen I spoke of earlier – was recognizably his own. That sheen was like something which had been polished over and over again. It didn't give forth light; it was like the moon, a reflected light.

Kreisler's tone was all sunlight, warm enough to melt your heart. The Heifetz sound was a much colder light, so nearly perfect that at times you could mistake it for a cosy log-fire. But it wasn't a log-fire: there were no ashes, no embers; there was no nostalgia. It was more akin to an electric current. Power and heat, as well as smoothness and a beguiling quality – all were in evidence, but somehow at a few degrees remove. Some people might be tempted to call his playing 'synthetic', but that wouldn't be fair because in all the world there was only one Heifetz.

Robin, do you remember the fairy tale about the fisherman and his wife?

RD: No; please remind me of it.

YM: Thanks to a series of magic wishes granted to the fisherman – by a fish which was in fact an enchanted prince – his wife decided they should move from their vinegar-jug home to a hut. But that wasn't good enough for her, so they moved to a mansion. There was no limit to her ambitions. Her wish to become queen was granted, then empress, and then Pope! Finally she brought disaster on herself by wanting to be like God, and she and her husband had to return to their vinegar jug.

I have related this fairy tale to you because, when I was a child, I was rather like the fisherman's wife. My ambitions were fired by listening to the superb recordings of Heifetz. I would then practise quite hard, but not yet with method, and I managed, as if by magic, to come somewhere near the Heifetz perfection. Eventually, like the fisherman's wife, I had to pay the price of ambitions too easily achieved. I had to start again at the beginning. I had to transform the intuitive ways of my childhood into a more conscious and analytic approach – not only to the musical score and its interpretation, but also to technique.

Heifetz always conveyed a sense of relaxation. He never hurried. At that time, especially when playing the more brilliant pieces in the repertoire, I was rather more impatient and wilful than Heifetz. He never gave the impression of being driven.

When he played the Beethoven – with that incredible discipline, remaining absolutely *a tempo* throughout the whole of the first movement, not giving himself or the music a chance to breathe freely, and yet always respectful towards the score – I found his interpretation lacking in some vital quality.

On the other hand, Heifetz played the Tchaikovsky with superb containment, a blend of reserve and domination. He didn't wallow in Tchaikovsky's music as some of his colleagues did, and as a few violinists do today. He didn't try to wring out of the concerto the very last drop of lusciousness. He gave it a sober and very dignified reading, in line with the true Russian interpretation of Tchaikovsky.

These days there is a tendency for sections of the art world to seek exaggerated effects. Instead of letting music speak with its natural voice, some performers force music to carry the burden of their own desire to excel, to make a big impression, to outdo their neighbour. The music then becomes more than itself, and at the same time less than itself. If music is allowed to flow from within itself, what it expresses is sufficient and completely convincing.

Striving for effects always has a false echo. I am thinking, for example, of those records, of sickening sweetness, that feature sixteen violins playing in harmony, high on the E string, with excessive *vibrato*. The result is like saccharin; just the opposite of the natural sweetness of fresh sugar cane, or of *aguamiel*, the juice from a Mexican cactus which drips overnight into a bucket and is then collected, before fermentation begins, to make one of the most delicious of all drinks.

A debasing aspect of the world today is the competitive element which oversells, shouts its wares, attracts attention by appealing to the lower instincts. The same set of values that produces over-glossy advertisements sometimes strays into music and the other arts. In this respect, Heifetz was a good example of how far one can go in technique and persuasiveness without crossing the threshold of bad taste.

Heifetz played the Tchaikovsky concerto with the same dignity and naturalness which you can hear in a Mravinsky rendering of a Tchaikovsky symphony: with a constant eye on the whole work, sensitively building the architecture of the music, with no exaggerated changes of *tempo*, and no swimming indulgence in each phrase.

I don't think Heifetz felt quite at home with the works of Bach, Mozart or Beethoven. Kreisler had an advantage here: coming from Austria, and having studied in Vienna, Paris and Rome, he had much more of a classical West European musical-artistic background than Heifetz. Heifetz did record the Bach solo sonatas, though I don't remember hearing them. He recorded the Elgar concerto and played it beautifully but very much in his own manner.

It is facile and unjust to call the playing of Heifetz 'slick'. I hate to hear people attack Heifetz and not give him any of the credit and respect he deserves. His gifts were a unique amalgam of the sense of timing and quality of presentation of a Jewish entertainer; the perfection of the competitive American stage; and the all-powerful Russian-Jewish desire for expression of emotion.

RD: I should be so glad if you would describe the presence of Kreisler on the concert platform. I picture him as a warm, attractive figure.

YM: Yes, always warm, always gentle. There was something of the lovable teddy-bear about Kreisler, with his grey hair and slight shuffle, which I think was the result of a wound from the First World War. His presence on the platform was benign. He was at one with his music and with his audience: everybody expected to be tenderly soothed and deeply moved. Kreisler had something wonderful to give, which his audience needed and were grateful for.

Heifetz, by contrast, came on to the platform in a cold, distant way. The embodiment of perfect concentration, he never took his eyes away from his left hand; he always held the violin high; apart from his arms, hands, and fingers, his body hardly moved when he was playing. It was difficult, almost impossible, to feel close to him as a person. You admired his performance and that was all. But with Kreisler, everybody was in love. He communicated love and he received love in return.

RD: Are there any musicians you learned from at a distance, people you never came to know personally?

YM: Certainly Chaliapin, whom I heard only twice in Paris when I was a boy, in *Prince Igor* and *Boris Godunov*. I was greatly impressed by this giant of a man. I imagine that Ysaÿe must have been similar to Chaliapin: both conveyed such power, such stature, such emotion, making all around them, however gifted, look like pygmies. Kreisler, despite all his charm, and Heifetz, despite his near-perfection, would have been overshadowed by Ysaÿe.

I met Ysaÿe once. From that meeting, and from all that I have been told about him, I am sure he had an incredible command on the concert platform, as well as elegance and a sense of *space*. In his indulgences, also, he was superhuman. A dozen bottles of beer presented no great challenge to him, and he was reported to be able to eat a whole leg of lamb at one sitting. Chaliapin, too, had a tremendous appetite, and this probably caused his downfall. Everything about Ysaÿe and Chaliapin was on a grand scale.

Enesco came near to Ysaÿe in command and stature of performance. When Enesco played the violin or sat down at the piano and played a keyboard transcription of an opera, you had *everything* before you. There would be much more missing at a fully-fledged Covent Garden production than there would be in listening to Enesco at an upright piano playing *Tristan*. When you came into Enesco's presence, you were in the presence of a complete world.

Enesco influenced me in many ways – by his spontaneity, his always generous nature, and his sense of freedom. His was the kind of freedom which, like a firework, soars, glows, and sparkles. It is so important today to remember that wholesome exuberance is an essential part of life. We are in danger of being satisfied with substitutes for natural release of feelings, in a life dictated more and more by machines and timetables. Trains – and here I am not necessarily talking about Britain! – have to arrive at 2:35, because

'Enesco was igniting.'

another train arrives at 2:34, and yet another at 2:36.

In so many aspects of daily living, we are being forced to enmesh into a coherent web more and more people, more and more factors; whereas in times past things could be allowed to happen in their own way and at their own pace. We are being robbed of our spontaneity.

In the barnstorming days, a musician would come to a town, put up his placards, and then wait and see who would turn up. If the first night was a success, the manager of the theatre would arrange for a few more concerts during the next week or two. Paganini did this. And so did the three Cherniavsky brothers, in Australia and elsewhere, not more than seventy years ago. It was perfectly possible to tour in that way. Communications in those days were not very good, and methods of travel were not reliable. You couldn't tell exactly when you would arrive. All you could do was promise to arrive sometime during the season, perhaps in month X, perhaps in month Y.

Did I ever tell you about my first concerts in Paris? They were booked in just this *ad hoc* way. I arrived in Paris, a boy of ten, and was introduced to Paul Paray, conductor of the Lamoureux Symphony Orchestra. He liked my playing and said right away, 'Next week I want you to play the *Symphonie espagnole*, and the Tchaikovsky a week later.' Imagine my arriving today in New York or Paris and offering to play next week! The impresario would say: 'We can't fit you in for at least two years.'

That illustrates the difference between now and earlier times. Enesco in his day was able to do what he wanted, when he wanted, to suit himself and those around him. He loved playing the violin, he loved playing chamber music, and he loved being with friends. His whole life was exuberant. There was little, so far as I know, that from one day to another contradicted his basic impulses. Chaliapin no doubt lived in much the same way.

But make no mistake, they worked hard. Enesco told me that on tour he would overhear Ysaÿe practising for hours and hours. These great musicians didn't gain or preserve their reputation without daily discipline.

Rubinstein is the last example of the exuberant, self-directed rhythm of life I have been talking about. At the age of eighty he would bound on to the platform and play very beautifully – not just one concerto, but often two or even three. Then he would stay up all night talking with his friends.

RD: Perhaps for a moment we can go beyond music. As a young person, who were your heroes – living, historical, fictional, mythical?

YM: Like every other American boy, and indeed like people all over the world, my great hero was Charles Lindbergh. To make the first non-stop solo flight across the Atlantic was at that time an adventure of storybook quality.

Among men of Biblical times, I admired David for his clean sense of obligation and for his courage.

The *Song of Solomon* is a book I have always adored. Solomon seemed to me the most complete of men, wise, loving and poetic. He was a king and yet he was worldly; he loved women and appreciated beauty; he must have been very witty; and he was *original*, in thought and action.

The life of Jesus gives me continuing inspiration. He advocated the fraternity of all human beings. He preached the doctrine of turning the other cheek, yet he never lacked courage or vigour – for example when he overturned the tables of the moneylenders, and drove them out of the temple with a scourge.

Of all the great artists, Leonardo da Vinci was my hero of heroes. He was not only a painter; he was also a sculptor, musician, poet, epigrammatist, architect, scientist, inventor, military engineer and town planner. An extraordinary man.

My parents had the very sound idea that holidays should never be wasted, and in the mid-Thirties I was taught Russian by a remarkable philologist, Lozinski, who used to learn a new language every year. He gave me a little book, beautifully illustrated, containing Leonardo's epigrams in Italian. To my lasting regret, I lost this charming book many years ago. I wish I had carried it with me everywhere.

Later on, I was much influenced by the writings of Constantin Brunner, a German Jew who was captured by the Nazis when Holland was over-run. He died in a gas chamber.

In 1938 a set of his books was sent to me anonymously; presumably by devoted friends of his who rightly guessed that Brunner's writings would interest me. I never met him, but after the war someone gave me a letter in which he had mentioned me.

Brunner's philosophy owed much to eastern thought and also to Spinoza, whom I very much admire. But at the same time Brunner's writings are thoroughly Germanic. He wrote the most beautiful prose. He was proud of the German language, which lends itself so naturally to philosophy and

Opposite: The young Menuhin with Ernest Bloch, whose last works were dedicated to him.

abstract thought. It took me several weeks to enter into the rhythm of his style, but from then on I read and read. His philosophy gave me a theoretical framework within which I could fit the events and experiences of life, and this framework continues to serve me.

The main theme in Brunner's work is an all-encompassing conception of life, in some way akin to the ancient Buddhist way of perceiving the atom. All those centuries ago they conceived of matter as being divisible into infinitely small particles. I read somewhere that the early Buddhists actually estimated the number of nerve ends in the spine. And their view of life ranged from the micro to the cosmic.

Brunner was one of the first to bridge the organic and the inorganic, a theory which is gradually gaining acceptance. He postulated that all creation – whether a stone, a leaf, a tree, an animal, or a human being – is animated and inhabited by an all-pervading being. All belong to one living process. He doesn't draw an arbitrary line anywhere.

There is nothing dry about his writings: his prose is notable for its intensity, its love, and its clarity. For example he wrote a passionate book called *Our Christ*; he worshipped Jesus, not as a God but as the greatest of the prophets.

Of all the philosophers I have read, Brunner comes nearest to my own intuitive conception of life. He manages to resolve apparent paradoxes and discrepancies in life: between people, between nations, between man and the infinite. His writings helped to clarify my thoughts at a time when I was looking for a general field theory, which would enable me to navigate my life with some sense of direction, and assess events as they were happening.

I was then in my early twenties and fortunately had enough time to read. Now I have so many obligations, and it has been some years since I have read any of his books. But I remain a faithful member of the Brunner Society and do what I can: I helped to have his books republished in Germany; they had been burned by the Nazis. There is now a Brunner Institute in The Hague, and, thanks to reprints and translations, I am glad to say that his works are becoming more widely known, understood, and valued.

RD: Perhaps we can now turn from the influence of philosophy to the influence of fiction. Have there been characters in novels, of any language, that you have been fond of or felt identified with?

YM: I have read relatively few novels. I enjoyed reading Mark Twain when I was a boy; and Willa Cather, a friend of the family, who had a lovely style. Later, *War and Peace* made quite an impression on me. I have read a few of Balzac's novels and some Dickens: *Martin Chuzzlewit*, *Nicholas Nickleby*, *Oliver Twist*, and *Bleak House*. I regard Dickens as the most *human* of all portrayers of people.

RD: You spoke of lacking time, at this stage in your life, for sustained reading. What are the books you like to dip into now and then?

YM: Lao Tzu mostly, and a few of Shakespeare's sonnets. I have just finished reading Irving Howe's *Immigrant Jews of New York, 1880–1922*, a fascinating book, but not one I would dip into for refreshment of the soul.

I love poetry that has a passionate living quality. I like Donne, Marvell and Victor Hugo. And I feel particularly close to Hölderlin and Goethe. Among my favourite poems of Goethe is *Blessed Longing* from a verse cycle based on eastern lyrics.

I first became acquainted with Hölderlin when I was about sixteen, thanks to my tutor Pierre Bertaux. Although selection is difficult, I am especially fond of *Hyperion's Song of Fate*; *Home*, which speaks of the juxtaposition of joy and pain; *Often while still a boy*, which begins with these lines:

> *Often while still a boy*
> *A god saved me*
> *From the shouts and rods of men;*

Middle of Life, with its splendid second verse:

> *Where shall I find, when*
> *Winter comes, flowers, and where*
> *Sunshine,*
> *And the shadows of earth?*
> *The walls will stand*
> *Speechless and cold; in the wind*
> *Weathervanes clatter;*

and lastly *To the Fates*, which begins:

> *A single summer grant me, Almighty Ones,*
> *And a single autumn for mellow song . . .*

and ends:

> *... for once I shall have*
> *Lived as the gods live, and that will suffice.*

To the Fates speaks to me of the artist's total commitment to his muse: he is willing to sacrifice everything in order to create and communicate his ideal, in all its range and depth.

RD: As you look back, what were the advantages and disadvantages of having been educated privately?

YM: Educated privately, I was able to have plenty of time for the violin, learn a few languages, and read whatever books my parents recommended. On the other hand, I missed the experience that comes from a large variety of subjects.

There are still many subjects I know very little about, such as mathematics and the sciences. But my lack of a school curriculum was compensated for in many ways. My father kept me informed about current events; my mother, about literature; and both my parents have a broad conception of humanity. Also, I have been fortunate enough to travel a good deal and meet people who filled some of the gaps in my education.

One vital experience I missed was the opportunity of, as it were, measuring myself, in the living moment, alongside other children. Instead, I was a law unto myself and my family, which was rather isolating – and frightening, because not until a long time afterwards did I feel at ease with people of my own age.

In the best schools, such as the English public school, you are, for the most part, master of your own time: you have to get work completed by agreed deadlines, but no one is looking over your shoulder, scheduling each step.

In complete contrast with this, I was brought up in the bosom of family life. Every day was ordered, and every hour within the day was ordered – but not by me. My life was ruled by the master timetable. That continued until I was almost twenty.

When I decided it was time to be on my own, I experienced a vacuum, a great void, because all at once I had to rely entirely on my own devices. My parents never interfered with that decision, in fact they encouraged it. The decision was relatively easy to take, but difficult to fulfil: I had so much ground to make up, in freely-chosen experience, in being totally responsible for myself.

As a child, I had never really been responsible for myself, and that, as I look back, was a disadvantage. Nevertheless there were advantages in my upbringing. There was no waste of time; I had my own sphere of responsibility, for the music I was practising, and for the concerts I gave; I was blessed with extraordinarily good parents and sisters, so that my days were never deprived or narrow or unadventurous, and I knew intimately the difficulties and rewards of family life.

There was plenty of diversion, but I was never able to give full flight to my desire for independence: I was always geared to the family. In many ways that was a good and healthy thing, a privilege; but disadvantages showed up subsequently, in many situations which I might have been able to handle better if I had had wider experience.

I am very grateful for my travels, and for all that I learned during the war: this helped to broaden me. I was already married, but I was still only half-developed. Now I was on my own, playing for our troops in many parts of the world, and I *had* to communicate. I had to say something to these men through music, and it was a very stimulating and salutary experience for me.

Music and the violin are a great protection. Always having that refuge has meant that mine has been a *charmed* life: I haven't had to fight my way as so many people have to. No doubt others have learned by their struggles – to earn enough money, to gain career advancement – and are thereby richer in some ways than I am, and more experienced.

My life and upbringing have had advantages and disadvantages. I have already paid the price for many of the disadvantages, though whether I have caught up completely I don't know. If I descended by parachute on to a country unknown to me, without my violin, with no money, and unable to speak the local language, I don't know how long I could survive. That would be a real test – one that I am not particularly keen to try!

2

THE VIOLIN

RD: What is there about the violin that has inspired you to accord it a lifetime of devotion?

YM: When I first asked for a violin there was no process of reasoning, no long and involved analysis. So often we look at the past only from our present viewpoint and this leads to unreasonable assumptions. I was a child who wanted to study the violin.

The children at my school, keen as they are to become musicians, haven't asked themselves in a deliberate way, 'Are we going to give our lives to our instruments?' That is not the way it happens.

There must be a logical basis for a child's wish or decision but the reasons are buried in the depths of time and in the influence, hidden but powerful, of forbears. Every aspect of heritage and environment contributes towards a child's inclination. In my case I owe much to the fact that my parents are Russian–Jewish. My father comes from the Chassidic sect, people who loved dancing and singing and playing the violin; my mother also loved music.

They took me to concerts when I was a small child and intuitively I reached out for an instrument that I sensed would be able to express my feelings. So at that stage I sought out the violin not so much for the purpose of playing to an audience, but simply to fulfil my need to find an outlet for my emotions. I felt sure I was making the right choice, and ever since I have been grateful to that early inclination of mine.

I doubt if I could have been really good at anything other than music. I've never given anything else much of a chance, but I'm interested in a thousand things. Maybe I could have been a good beekeeper or a good doctor, I don't know. I certainly am *fascinated* by the human condition, the human body, the human mind, the human spirit. I might have made a good pastor but, considering that I find my errant life interesting and adventurous, I'm sure I would have found work in a parish rather confining.

What leads us to the choice of a partner? And what are the chances of a marriage lasting? Whether or not we can fulfil our vows 'until death us do

part' depends on our hopes, our deepest imaginings, our mistakes, our view of society's conventions, and on the course our own life, and that of those close to us, takes. Many people seem to have an anticipation of failure. The other day I heard a joke about this: 'Oh Mummy, I would like my *first* marriage to be a success!'

The violin is in a sense a life partner. Although I haven't always played the same instrument, I have remained married to the violin in a symbolic way. Even now I like experimenting with a different instrument from time to time in the search for new sound, new stimulus. Another violin, if it is a fine one, a Guarnerius or a Strad, can add to the zest and excitement of playing, but for most of the time I remain faithful to my favourite Strad.

RD: Do you observe any particular differences in temperament which prompt one child to choose the violin and another the piano?

YM: The child who chooses the violin wants to hear a single voice – another aspect of his own voice, perhaps – and may have a lonely or at least individualistic personality, one that asks many questions and wants a very particular kind of answer. This temperament is *quite* different from the more global, in a way more harmonic, inclinations of the pianist. To a pianist, tone quality may mean a little less, though he too must search for a beautiful sound. The preoccupation with a harmonic score, with the movement of many voices, with a keyboard that is not perfectly in tune, can be a more intellectual pursuit, though it need not be: there are plenty of passionate pianists.

Because the pianist is not *creating* the note, he probably needs to be able to *see* more, behind the sound he achieves by hitting the keys, for that sound to be acceptable intellectually; whereas, conversely, the sound you make on a violin when you first start is far less tolerable than the sound you make on a piano.

Many musicians play the violin and the piano. My first teacher, Louis Persinger, played both instruments very well, and at my school we have had several young people who play both. For example we had a very talented boy from Singapore, Yit Kin Seow, who is now making a career as a pianist. But for several years, while he was still studying and playing the piano, he guested as a viola player with one or two leading orchestras.

The violin seems to me more human, more intimate, more like a voice calling. Playing the piano may have less of *flight* than playing the violin, though it can display this quality in the hands of a great pianist.

When Bach composed *The Art of Fugue* he didn't have any particular instrument in mind. It is, quite simply, wonderful counterpoint, and is suitable for string instruments, piano, organ, perhaps even for a choir. At the highest level of performance and of dedication to music, all instruments become equals.

RD: What is your attitude these days to practice?

YM: I *love* practice. I don't practise nearly as much as I'd like to because I have so many other demands on my time. For me, practice is a period of exploration, of renewing sensations. The tactile element in violin playing is very strong because – unlike the piano, for which touch is also most important – everything changes continually. No octave is the same distance as another octave. Intonation is not fixed. There is no single note or sound which is always the same. The *infinite* subtleties of tone production, depending on the *slightest* inflections and changes in pressure and speed and position, are so great that it is quite out of the question to master each one separately.

You have to master a range of sound, you have to master an area. When a country is taken over, it is conquered all at once or area by area, not inch by inch. With the violin you perceive the whole space and range, from the greatest pressure to the smallest, from the fastest speed to the slowest, from the lowest position to the highest. All these elements interact with your awareness and use of the body and of parts of the body, from tightness to looseness, from resistance to yielding, heavy to light, giving you myriads of possibilities which you use intuitively as you play, as you feel.

Violin playing is a live process, never twice the same, and yet there can be a methodical approach which, more and more, I realize is primarily an approach of subtlety and not of attack. Power and attack – in the musical sense of that word – come as a result of balance and a sense of finesse, being aware of the smallest possible differences. Once you have established your range in all respects – speed, weight, placing and so on, range of *vibrato* from widest to narrowest, from slow to fast – your ability to create the kind of sound you want, whether you are playing down-bow or up-bow, should come naturally.

It is an extraordinary fact that, as you play, your intention is translated into minute movements not only of your fingers but of muscles in the back. In that way I suppose violin playing is no different from any other craft or skill: the artist's intention goes straight into the cutting edge of his knife or the stroke of his brush.

3

INTERPRETATION AND PERFORMANCE

RD: Please will you describe how your conception of the Beethoven concerto, which I know you prize above all others, has evolved over the years.

YM: From my boyhood on – given that I could play the violin reasonably well – I have always been able to *feel* the Beethoven concerto. I know what I want it to convey. I know the contained power and dignity it has. Even as a child, thanks to my teachers, Persinger and Enesco, the *meaning* of the work never eluded me. Later, by conscious analysis, I set up the structural scaffolding which I needed – to justify, as it were, what I had already known more intuitively. I was then able to play the Beethoven with perhaps more authority; not necessarily with more conviction.

My interpretation of the Beethoven has had a subtle evolution, as you suggest, throughout the years. It hasn't taken any great leaps forward: the road I started on is the road I continue to follow. This has led me, in a natural progression, to other works of Beethoven because so much of one's accumulated experience can be transferred from one of his works to another. For example, a scale is much more than the word 'scale' might imply: each of its notes carries abundant meaning. In Beethoven's music a scale or an *arpeggio* is always symbolic, always intensely important, an integral part of the overall design.

Today I believe I can play the Beethoven concerto better than I have played it in the past, largely because the music has become much more part of me: in some ways clearer and more explicit, and yet just as full of wonder and mystery. I have never taken the Beethoven for granted. The beginning of the *larghetto* or the entrance of the strings in the first movement, when the violins repeat D sharp – these are moments which fill me with awe and astonishment.

As a child, my performance gained unity through my intuition. Now logic has been added to that intuitive approach; I have gone through the period when I asked so many questions of myself and of the score. The wonder, the

43

newness, the haunting originality – they all continue alongside the growing familiarity. But this is not the familiarity that breeds contempt. Quite the contrary. For me, familiarity with anything or anyone increases the wonder.

Now when I hear the *timpani* begin with that quietly insistent phrase, and the woodwind answer, establishing the key of D major, I am transported in a way that I wasn't as a child, when the music seemed more matter-of-fact than it does now. I have lived through so much in these last years. Perhaps the sublime simplicity of the opening and its basic pulse now take on more meaning, more weight of experience, and therefore more humanity.

I now know what I want the opening to express. I know what I expect of the orchestra when I play or conduct, and this is something more than just the notes, which might have done good service in the past, had they merely been in tune and in time. And I know what atmosphere or mood I should like the audience to feel: a message of equilibrium, a serenity which survives the early doubts cast by the string entry and becomes affirmation.

Beethoven has a fondness for eruption, for sudden changes from *pianissimo* to *fortissimo*, and for those extraordinary pauses – so suggestive, so full of life and meaning – in which the music continues through the silence. All these fingerprints of his style mean more to me symbolically than they did before.

My enduring affection for the Beethoven is rather like what I might feel towards a keepsake: it grows more precious with the passing of years; it accumulates importance through a subtle kind of companionship and mutual trust.

RD: Do you get new insights about a particular work, or about teaching, or about any aspect of your musical life, when you are completely away from music?

YM: Yes, I do. I have always been doubtful about the head-on approach to any problem; I find the strategy of the side attack much more valuable. Very often what I am working on makes more progress if I leave it and do something else for a while and then return. Even if I stop playing altogether for three or four days, what I was working on previously will have taken new shape. This doesn't mean that the time between periods of work is more important than the time of the work itself; we need both. Whatever the project, we have to undergo a period of effort, and sometimes of struggle, and then there is a time of absorption, of assimilation, of organic integration

INTERPRETATION AND PERFORMANCE

within, when what we have been seeking becomes part of us.

There is a vast difference between doing something intellectually, wilfully, deliberately, and, as it were, being *acted upon*. When we play music, the process is as much creatively passive as it is active.

RD: As someone once said, 'Our dreams dream us.'

YM: Yes, exactly. I agree entirely with that. But for dreams to dream us the way we would like them to, we must prepare them up to a point. For example, if we go to see a vicious film, full of violence and all kinds of degraded human behaviour, we will probably have nightmares; and we will have brought them upon ourselves. It is rather like suffering from stomach-ache after eating too much. We've earned, deserved, the stomach-ache and have to put up with it. We are stomach-ached! At that stage we are a passive sufferer, but we would have prevented the stomach-ache had we not overeaten.

My ideal, when playing the violin, or teaching, or talking, or walking, is that I should be played, taught, talked, walked. I want to be an active recipient. I would love to be one of those doctors – and I know two or three – who take an all-embracing view: who know their job, and medicine, so well; who understand a human being spiritually and psychologically as well as physically; who take into account the effect, on the patient, of heredity and environment and the time of day, the patient's body rhythm. Both the doctor and the musician need to be aware of so many different elements of such an incredibly diverse nature.

A doctor may in the past have studied each element separately, but in his consulting room, when he is seeing a patient and trying to formulate a diagnosis, all these elements are being activated and are so infinitely complex to unravel that they would challenge the powers of a computer. The really skilled doctor meets his patient and allows all his accumulated knowledge and insight to come into play as he carries out his examination, noticing the shape and movements of the body, the reflection of light on the skin, and a thousand other revealing characteristics. That is the kind of doctor – and teacher – I should like to be.

The other day at my school I noticed that I was teaching a few young children with much more clarity, naturalness and precision than ever before. I was able to diagnose a problem and make certain points absolutely clear to a nine-year-old girl; and we did it laughingly. The second and third fingers of her left hand were not acting independently. I began by saying, 'Perhaps you can tell us what is wrong.' She was hesitant, so I said, 'If you have two objects that you want to be able to move freely and to control and direct, can they move more easily if they are rubbing against each other or if they are separated?' 'If they are separated,' she replied. 'All right,' I said, 'now look at your fingers. Why are they together? If you are making a basic mistake, no one is going to blame you. It is simply that you haven't been able to analyse the problem. You can correct it once you have seen the problem and tried out different positions of hand and fingers in exercises without the violin. Each finger wants to be able to move independently. To achieve this, there must be no resistance in any of the other joints. They must act in support and co-operation.'

I like to reduce a problem to a very simple equation and then find its links with a wider view of life. From my work with this little girl, an image or model could be built which would be applicable to the whole of society. An individual needs to be integrated into a collective system and at the same time feel free and independent. He can't feel free if he is held back by an arbitrary kind of restraint. And so also with a violinist's left hand: for each finger to be able to respond freely, all the joints need to react in co-ordination.

I try to establish relationships between my two worlds: my knowledge of the fingerboard and a general experience of life. One view is confined to an area of only a few square inches; the other is open to the universe. I often discover that there are valid and straightforward principles common to both, to do with friction; the use of power; the analysis of problems, from the intuitive to the deliberate, rational approach; balance; freedom and the impediments to freedom, one's own and society's – namely, prejudice, illusion, selfishness, greed.

I like to make these basic equations. I hope that the children I teach will grow up with an understanding that personal liberty can be likened to the freedom of the joints of their fingers. If the joints are rigid, they will impede thoughts, emotions and impulses, that want to be expressed.

When we watch a violinist, we judge by the fingers because they are the end-product of the will. It is the fingers that move on the strings and handle the bow, but what often escapes both the observer and the player is the use of the rest of the body. I see students giving attention to the use of their fingers when what they should be working at is the continuity between the fingers, knuckles, wrist, elbow, shoulders, and the upper and lower parts of the back.

The freedom of the head is another problem. So I suggest to the children

that they start off not with a tense effort to play, to make sound, but rather with a feeling of being able to move on the fingerboard with no tension. I also suggest that they simply be aware of the balance of the head, without even allowing the chin to touch the chin rest, or the shoulder to touch the violin; bending the body in such a way that the violin is lightly balanced on the collar bone.

Of course if you work with people who are prejudiced, narrow-minded, determined that they are right, blind to any other opinion, then it is very difficult to achieve a harmonious outcome. But the principles of harmony – of thought, of behaviour, and of sound – permeate the whole of my school's community, children and teachers alike. The tone and atmosphere in the school is like a piece of music. That is not my doing; it is thanks to the calibre of person who is attracted to the school and to the dedicated work they do there.

So many people have to live their lives without seeing the results of what they have done. But at the school we have a community that is working together, and they all have the elation of hearing, experiencing, the results of their endeavours. The staff can see and hear every day – by their manner, their gait and the sounds they make – the children's satisfaction in achieving what *they* have achieved. For all of us on the staff, this gives us many new thoughts about teaching, and is a constant source of inspiration and of renewed dedication.

RD: You've been talking about youth and achievement in music, and I am reminded of something my teacher, Alan Rowlands, said when we were studying one of the Beethoven piano concertos. He said that great maturity and inner confidence are needed in order to play really slowly in a public performance.

YM: That is true. The player needs to be aware of his own inner pulse. If you are dependent on audience reaction or on extraneous comment, you won't gain this state of serenity. But if you do have it, then the audience, by profound listening, by holding its breath, during a slow, soft, extended passage, will enhance your feeling of poise and self-containment: you'll be aware of holding a vast audience in a kind of magical suspense. Such a moment comes in the middle of the slow movement of the Beethoven violin concerto when nobody in the audience dares to move. An accomplished Indian musician improvising on the sitar can create a similar atmosphere.

Of all the world's orchestras, the Berlin Philharmonic is probably the one that can play slowest with conviction. Of course they are able to play very fast passages with great precision, but they leave each note with regret. They give quality, validity and beauty of tone to every note, every chord. The Berlin players have the advantage of having played Beethoven more often with great conductors than any other orchestra; and the epic length and proportions of the German classical repertoire has bred exceptional patience among the players. The best Russian orchestras also display this quality, appearing to have endless space and time. The French on the other hand tend to be more mercurial, more suited to economical statement, to the perfect miniature.

The German has a natural gift for philosophy, but he is inclined to weave abstractions, and penetrate into endless new, and sometimes bizarre, vistas of the mind; in so doing, he can cut himself off from life and then the beat of the tomtom of reality doesn't seem to reach him. But the Berlin Philharmonic is an example of the Germanic at its best: never dry; able to produce a wonderfully rich sound. I never cease to be amazed by the way the young players who have been drafted into the orchestra in recent years preserve the spirit and traditions of Nikisch and Furtwängler.

RD: The harpsichordist Kenneth Gilbert said recently, 'To be a performer, you have to be an exhibitionist.' How would you respond to that?

YM: I don't think it is necessarily true. Music, and indeed all the fine arts, and the traditional crafts as well, allow scope for every conceivable temperament and personality type: I dislike the paintings of Francis Bacon, I couldn't bear to have any of them in my house, and yet I acknowledge him as a gifted painter.

Performance and exhibitionism have some relationship, but I have known some very great artists who were very introvert, pianists who almost hid behind their piano. By contrast there are of course pianists – and violinists! – who are flamboyant.

Of the children at my school, some are very extrovert, others not at all. We have a boy, now in his teens, who is very intelligent, brilliant at physics and electronics, and a fine violinist. He plays the Honegger solo sonata incredibly well, but he ends the piece carelessly, almost as if he were ashamed of his performance. I think that someone who plays as well as he does should end with strength and authority, so as to form a natural link between his

performance and the audience reaction.

Much depends of course on the way a work concludes. If it ends *pianissimo*, there is no scope for a final flourish; instead you try to finish in such a way that the music will linger in the mind and memory of the audience, and then in their own time they will show their appreciation. But if a brilliant piece ends with a thundering assertion, it is a pity to belie that assertion by letting your bow drop as if neither you nor the music had conveyed anything.

RD: It is one thing to play Bach; it is another thing to play Sarasate! Do different composers bring out different parts of your personality?

YM: Yes, certainly. I have always played and conducted a wide range of music, from Strauss waltzes to Grappelli jazz, from improvisations with Ravi Shankar to Beethoven, Sarasate, and even vulgar display pieces. I like them all and I think they all have their place.

RD: When you played on the same concert platform as a great composer – Elgar, Britten, Enesco – did you feel a special atmosphere, respond to a special inspiration?

YM: Yes. Ben was usually very nervous before a public performance. Why he should have been, God only knows, because there was no more superb pianist or conductor. Some of the greatest musical moments I have known were when playing with Ben or listening to him accompanying Peter Pears in a song cycle such as Schubert's *Die Winterreise*. Whatever music Ben touched came alive in a new way, even Beethoven, whose music he wasn't especially fond of; for example he played beautifully in the 'Geister' Trio. Ben's nervousness affected him terribly before a concert but didn't adversely affect his performance: once he was making music he was completely at one with himself.

Elgar on the other hand was quite unaffected by nerves before or during a

Opposite: Friendship and mutual respect link two disciplines: Menuhin with jazz violinist Stephane Grappelli.

Overleaf: Collaborating with Elgar on the historic first recording of his violin concerto in 1932.

To dear Yehudi in memory [...] delightful time we had recording [...] concerto last May. [...]

concert. He was always natural and unselfconscious, whether conducting in front of a large audience or sitting in his armchair at home. I didn't notice that he was ever visibly or emotionally altered by the occasion. Neither was Enesco; he was always a passionate musician, but on the platform he was completely *in* the music and was the most wonderful accompanist.

As an accompanist you must forget yourself and listen acutely to your colleague and therefore you cannot afford to be an altered personality when on the platform. Your reactions may from time to time be heightened, sharper, more attuned, but not fundamentally altered.

There can be moments, and I have experienced them, of nervousness at a concert. This may happen if I am playing a work for the first time in public and have not completely absorbed the new score; or if I am not in the best physical or mental condition, perhaps because of worry about a family matter. But most of the great artists I have known have walked naturally and easily on and off the platform, and have simply been themselves while playing.

RD: In your career have there been any marked differences, for good or bad, between rehearsal and performance?

YM: Yes, there have. Of course it is ideal when the rehearsal is good and the concert is still better, but I have known a fair number of times when the opposite has happened. When I was younger, I never liked repeating myself. Perhaps there was some kind of self-proving, self-justification, in this. If I played at the rehearsal the way I wanted to play, that became for me *the* performance of the day, and I looked upon the concert in the evening as just a repetition. But I haven't felt that for a number of years.

Quite often in the past I used to be keyed-up for the morning's rehearsal. Then I might have a rest in the afternoon. So a difference between rehearsal and performance might have been in part due to a physiological change. Diana often used to tease me and say: 'I don't want to hear that the rehearsal was better than the concert.' Now I have evolved a much more reliable routine for the day of a performance. On the whole I no longer find that by evening I have spent myself emotionally, or that physically I am not as robust as I had been earlier in the day.

RD: We've been talking about the potential difference between rehearsal and performance, and I'd very much like to hear your views on your

Rehearsing with Britten: 'He possessed genius.'

conception of a work *vis-à-vis* the reality of playing. I remember your speaking about this at the Royal College in the mid-Sixties.

YM: At best there is a reciprocal heightening of conception and performance: thus the performance leads to a wider conception, and a new conception leads to a better performance. There should be no great discrepancy between the two. That is the goal.

The conception is not disembodied, not an abstraction. Rather it is something which an instrumentalist feels in his fingers, and is conditioned by the sound he hears; and he must never compromise his conception if the sound he hears is *less* than his conception.

Players sometimes lower their standards by rationalizing, saying to themselves, 'Well, this is probably the way it will have to be,' and then they begin to accept a lower level of performance. There is, I suppose, a defeatist, compromising element lurking in most of us.

I like to think that I *renew* my conception by re-studying an already familiar work, using my imagination to search out its meaning, and thus keeping alive my *vision* of the music. Also, if it is a great work, performance will *enhance* not only the conception but also the technical means at my disposal, and the variety of tone colour, and the assurance I bring to my playing. All this enables the work to seem to be growing continually. It is surprising how much the conception depends on and responds to technical capacity. A combination of increased assurance of technique and the higher demands made by a heightened conception enable a player to take risks he would never dare attempt otherwise.

RD: That reminds me of one of Schnabel's favourite injunctions to his pupils: 'Safety last.'

YM: On the whole I regard that as a good injunction. Certainly a performer ought to be ready to take a risk, let things happen *to* him, surrender himself to a measure of abandon. If you have prepared the music thoroughly and if you trust your intuition, the element of conviction in your performance will come not from care or hesitancy but from abandonment. If your playing is rather too abandoned, you may occasionally make a scratchy sound, and you may not hit every note exactly in the middle; on the other hand, being careful gives *no* guarantee of accuracy. None at all.

RD: Something else Schnabel said, this time in later life, was that he only wanted to play music which was better than it could be performed.

YM: I can hear his critical colleagues substituting the words, 'better than *he* could perform it!'

I would never want to concede that, theoretically at least, a performance cannot measure up to the greatness of the music. But I would be the first to admit when my own performance of a particular work falls short.

What Schnabel – to do him justice – might have had in mind is that because a great work has so *many* possibilities of interpretation, no single 'reading' can reveal the music in all its facets.

Another angle on Schnabel's statement occurs to me. Just as I might under-rate the ability of someone I know – however resilient – to cope during a plague, a fire, or a war, so also I cannot visualize the full potential of a great piece of music. For instance I vividly remember hearing the Amadeus play Schubert's *Quintet with two cellos* at the funeral of a colleague of mine. In the poignancy of that occasion and that setting, the *Quintet* took on a new dimension for me, far more moving, far more potent, than anything I could previously have imagined.

RD: Conversely, are there any works which you were challenged by – both emotionally and technically – earlier in your career, but which no longer offer such a challenge?

YM: Yes. The first to come to mind is the Tchaikovsky concerto, a most engaging work but one which has been exploited. There is hardly a single violinist who hasn't tried to play it more beautifully, more lusciously, more brilliantly, than his colleagues. Thus the Tchaikovsky has been over-played, over-used, and yet it has been exceptionally well played more often than almost any other work in the standard repertoire. In content, it doesn't have the depth of many other violin concerti: it is not a work that seems to grow. This, combined with its over-exposure, has caused me to tire of it somewhat.

It is a curious fact that, with works that are so romantic, so over-played, violinists who are native-born – the Russians in the case of the Tchaikovsky concerto – play the music much more classically than others do. Whereas we in the west tend to use the Tchaikovsky as a vehicle for exaggeration and self-display, everyone trying to outdo the performances of his colleagues, the Russians play it much more soberly and with much more discipline; and the music loses nothing in power or effectiveness. That is an important lesson for every musician.

RD: You mentioned earlier that you have evolved a routine for the day of a concert. Supposing that tonight you were to play at the Albert Hall, what would be the pattern of your day?

YM: In my theoretical conception of the day of a concert, I never preclude the unexpected, the possibility of an obligation, such as a family illness or other emergency, which would have to take precedence over the concert.

Barring some such unwelcome event, I like to work quietly in the morning; unless I am on tour, in which case I am usually travelling in the morning. But if the concert was to be at the Albert Hall, I would get up at about seven o'clock, bathe, exercise and breakfast; warm up with the violin between eight and nine; and then go to the hall, arriving by 9.30 at the latest, so as to have at least half an hour to warm up before the rehearsal at ten.

If there is no rehearsal early in the day then I can order my morning a little more leisurely. I get up a bit later, look at the mail, and perform my usual morning ritual. This consists of washing and rubbing the body to get the circulation going, and a certain amount of exercise: slow and fast, heavy and light, inverted body postures, hanging by the arms and by the legs – all the variations I can think of. Each day they are different. I never repeat exactly the same series, but my favourite postures and the basic elements of movement are always included.

Then I practise for a while, an hour and a half or so, and perhaps go for a walk with my wife before lunch. I have a good sleep after lunch and then, at around four o'clock, do some more exercises to limber up the body.

At lunch I will have eaten fairly substantially – but only light food. I don't like to eat any meat on the day of a concert. I find I have more control, more relaxation, greater peace of mind and body, if I don't have meat. I don't like eating too much carbohydrate either, but I like rice, potatoes, and whole grains of every variety. I like vegetables and I love porridge; sometimes I have porridge at outlandish times of the day.

After I have done my exercises, I begin practising with the violin at about five o'clock. I prefer a concert at about 8.30 because it gives me more time to

Opposite: Rehearsing with von Karajan.

prepare. 7.30 is a bit of a rush: it means that, allowing for evening traffic, I have to leave Highgate by about 6.15.

Usually I will dress just before five o'clock, so as not to have to dress between my violin warming-up at five and the arrival at the hall: I like to diminish as far as possible the time *between* stopping practice at home and the beginning of warming-up at the hall. When I am on tour I usually aim to get to the hall an hour and a half before the concert. Then, regardless of what has taken place immediately before – travelling or seeing friends or being interviewed by journalists – at least I have one and a half hours clear and can work quietly by myself.

At about six o'clock, before I leave home, and usually also at the hall a little later, half an hour before I play, I take some nourishment, a tisane. It might be rose-hip tea or some other kind of herb tea into which I put a generous amount of Molat. Molat is a specially prepared powder consisting of essential nutrients. It has a high content of the B vitamins and of Lecithin.

Or I may have some Bio-strath, a Swiss preparation made from yeast culture. This too is rich in vitamin B. Sometimes I have Granoton which is wheat germ and rich in vitamin C. Then there are various capsules, one or two of which, now that I have reached the venerable age of sixty, are regenerative. I often take Ginseng in one of its various forms. I usually have honey and yeast powder too.

Of course I don't take all these preparations together: I choose at random from what is in my little concert-picnic-bag and mix everything into an unpalatable drink. I don't really care about the taste. The main thing is to have something warm and comforting, which will keep the circulation going, and overcome any signs of fatigue or strain. I never take any drugs or stimulants: I don't feel the need of them, and I like to be in full possession of all my faculties. I like to feel that whatever I do isn't helped by any artificial aid. The preparations I have mentioned are all natural-food extracts of the highest quality.

My special mixture gives me strength and calories – it is virtually a meal in itself – but it is easily digestible, giving me sustenance and energy without any accompanying heaviness.

Then I continue warming up. I dislike having any interruption between my warming up and my playing. I like to have plenty of time to prepare myself, in a quiet, relatively methodical way, and then walk on to the platform perfectly naturally.

A violinist, perhaps more than any other instrumentalist, dislikes having to give a performance when he is not fully played-in. Just walking in from the street and picking up the violin has never been my idea of the ideal. I like to go through my own sequence of stages. On the other hand, I know that life isn't always compliant. I have played directly after a train journey or while still suffering from 'flu, and during the war I played for the forces under every kind of circumstance imaginable.

RD: How responsive are you to the atmosphere of the city you are playing in and the audience you are playing to?

YM: I am quite conscious of atmosphere but this does not materially affect my performance – even if the audience were distinctly hostile. If I was really enjoying my performance, I would be too absorbed in it to be disturbed.

I equate a good performance with complete sway over the audience. I have never had the experience of playing the way I want to play and finding that the audience wasn't prepared to listen . . . on reflection, that isn't quite true. There have been a couple of exceptions. One was during the war, when an audience assembled without expecting to hear any music. I played in between two film shows, and so the people in the auditorium were taken by surprise, having set their minds on leaving the cinema or seeing the next film.

I recall another and different type of occasion, a concert in one of the suburban towns outside Chicago. The audience was docile and listened quietly, but they didn't seem to react, and I distinctly felt that I was playing to people who preferred to listen to music on the radio or television, and were frustrated because they couldn't turn a knob and find out what was on the other channels!

Apart from those few occasions, a concert audience has never disappointed me. And so I feel that enjoying my playing – and I cannot enjoy it unless I am playing well – is synonymous with an appreciative audience.

RD: Jacqueline du Pré, in a recent and most moving radio programme, said that a concert audience sends forth, as it were, an essence which the musician needs.

YM: I am sure she is right. Any public performance has a communal element. The audience is a group of people sharing similar emotions, with the soloist being the mouthpiece of that essential power which comes from the group. And a sense of excitement, and even elation, is reflected back on the music and the performer.

RD: I believe some recent research has demonstrated that the aura of a musician can change the mood or – to use the word in its original sense – the temper of an audience.

YM: Yes, they have managed to photograph the aura by using equipment that is sensitive to different degrees of vibration. All of us exude radiation, the source and nature of which has yet to be defined; but it definitely exists, and visual evidence has been produced. I have somewhere upstairs a photograph of a singer, showing these radiations. There is a three-way link between colour, the type and degree of radiation, and the state of mind of the person being photographed. The state of mind is definitely affected by music.

Some of the most original work in this field is being done by Manfred Clynes, an Australian pianist and scientist. He monitors the mind and mood of someone who is listening to music, with a device not unlike the original Morse-code transmitter. The extraordinary thing is that *all* listeners, from whatever social and educational background, produce a recognizably distinct and similar pattern for each composer. Thus there is a Beethoven curve, a Mozart curve, a Debussy curve and so on. Within these patterns changes of emotion are observable: a curve showing resignation, a curve of aggression, a curve of love. These secondary patterns correspond very closely with emotions expressed in the music.

Manfred Clynes has postulated a fascinating theory, which he calls the Sentic Cycle, showing how we go through a cycle of emotions, beginning with negative and even violent ones – suspicion, envy, hate, aggression – which have to be purged, spent, resolved, sublimated, before the more directly creative emotions – love, faith, reverence – can be experienced.

Dr Clynes has done a lot of work with patients, people suffering from worry and tension. He first takes them through the Cycle with music; after a time they can go through the Cycle themselves by auto-suggestion. They almost invariably emerge from this experience with more strength and confidence.

The Sentic Cycle does what every great work of literature and music does: having experienced a whole gamut of emotions, you feel cleansed. What are Handel's oratorios, the Mozart *Requiem* and Bach's great *Passions* but dramatic stories which take the listener through all kinds of emotion? In the Bach *Passions* we re-live Christ's betrayal and trial, the crown of thorns, the call of the crowd for him to be crucified; we journey from suspicion and hypocrisy to hope and final consolation. This is the musical equivalent of the Sentic Cycle, extended over a period of two or three hours.

Having seen men of philosophy and art lose their temper, and knowing that I am not in full control of my anger if I meet an officious or overbearing person, I ask myself what is adrenalin for? It is for our protection: to galvanize us to fight, to run away, or just to be on our guard. We cannot ignore the fact that our bodies produce many secretions linked to aggression, and one of the major problems of our time is the lack of acceptable outlets for these basic drives, generally untamed and undisciplined. Experiencing the Sentic Cycle is a way of absorbing and integrating emotions that are difficult to liberate when living in a so-called civilized community. After listening to the *St Matthew Passion* I feel like a wet cloth that has been wrung completely dry. I feel peaceful, restored, and I am sure the rest of the audience feels the same way.

The music of the east is totally different: it selects one mood or atmosphere to express, and can then maintain this for hours. There may be a certain rise in tension as the rhythms become more complex, but this is quite unlike western music's fast changes of mood. In a Beethoven symphony or quartet you experience, within only a few minutes, sudden and wide contrasts, from power to tenderness, from joy to sorrow. In life, joy and sorrow can and do alternate in close sequence; but much of western music tends to be very swift in its juxtaposition of emotions.

This is not the case with folk music: one piece will describe a dance or a wedding or mourning. And the sections of a Bach suite are very much centred around a single mood, a single key. The advent of romantic music, and the many trends and fashions which followed, brought not only denser harmony but also more intense emotional contrasts. Clynes's Sentic Cycle gives us a most helpful means of studying, analysing, and making therapeutic use of emotional sequence, both musical and psychological.

The Japanese have an exemplary capacity for emotional and bodily control. In activities such as ju-jitsu and their various forms of drama, they can switch with explosive speed from complete relaxation to sudden movement. To our way of perceiving, their movements do not form a smooth sequence and are rather like a succession of stills, instead of a motion picture at its normal speed.

With a westerner, you are aware of anger boiling up and of increasing loss of self-control; but those Japanese who are highly trained in their native arts are always relaxed, and always have a degree of detachment from whatever they are doing.

They are able to *will* their emotions. I have watched Japanese children sit completely engrossed in folding bits of paper into various shapes, such as animals: they are content to do this for hours at a time and never make a sound. I don't recall seeing western children of the same age show as much concentration as this. It is a very high form of discipline, but not brutal or destructive, because it is self-discipline, quietly pursued, and with a play element as well.

Menuhin's interests transcend national and cultural boundaries. Here he is making music with Ravi Shankar.

We in the west find it very difficult to relate to time and space. Empty space and empty time cause us terror. Our economy generates products to fill every possible gap. If you have five minutes free, you turn on the television, you read the newspaper, you use your camera, you pour yourself a drink, you get into your car and go somewhere, anywhere.

We also fill space in a compulsive way. If we have a gap in a corner of a room, we buy something to fill that gap. If we have an unused area in a big city, we build an office block. But the Japanese, even in their crowded island, keep space uncluttered. For example, their rooms are often small but always spacious: they will only display one or two beautiful objects at a time. And their beds don't take up any room: they can be rolled up and put into a closet during the daytime.

Whenever you want to rest, you unroll your soft, thin mattress on the *tatami*, which smells divinely of clean, finely-woven straw. The texture is almost silken and yet it has a springiness. They are lovely to walk on – either barefoot or when wearing soft, cloth slippers – and are used for covering most floors instead of carpets.

I greatly admire this idea of not cluttering, and of being able to be quiet for a given time, without asking anything, without necessarily giving anything – except the all-important unobtrusiveness you dedicate to your community. The Japanese have changed enormously under western, and particularly American, influence. But when I was there, immediately after the war, I saw quite a lot of the old Japan. It was then possible to be in the company of twenty people in a room and be almost unaware of them. You can hardly be unaware of a roomful of twenty Americans!

RD: A question occurs to me about presence of another kind. How large an ingredient is concentration in a public performer's presence which is felt by the audience to be strong, commanding, magnetic?

YM: There is a paradox here. An artist's presence is more strongly felt, the more he is concentrated, centred, and *dis*regarding the audience.

I don't want this to sound one-sided. You come before your audience with a feeling of warmth, friendliness and gratitude. Having bought their tickets, they have come with trust and faith in you, prepared to give you their time and awaiting with pleasure and expectation a gift, as it were, in return.

In addition to this attitude towards your audience, you have a most intimate relationship with your instrument and the music. The more absorbed

67

In the Sheldonian Theatre, Oxford. Conducting the Bath Festival Orchestra from the violin. 'The performer's rôle is to inspire.'

you are in the music – and thus the more you withdraw your presence from the audience – the more strongly they will feel your presence.

Ultimately, the attitude of an audience – either listening deeply or fidgeting and thinking of a hundred things apart from the music – depends on the soloist. Unless you set an example of complete dedication, the audience will have nothing to follow, nothing to emulate. The performer's rôle is to inspire the audience to follow him in his devotion, his devotional act.

That is the ideal. Sometimes, I confess, when the music is being played well enough, and there is a good *ambiance* on the platform, the artists' minds may wander.

That doesn't happen very often, but I remember one particular tour with Ferenc Fricsay, one of the finest conductors I have known. His conducting style was so aesthetically satisfying: fluent and precise, beautiful to watch. He was Hungarian, a pupil of Kodály, and began conducting while still a child. When Ferenc was seven or eight, his father told him to conduct one of his own brass bands, saying simply, 'Now go ahead. Conducting is your job too.'

We were on tour with the Radio Symphony Orchestra of Berlin for several weeks, giving a concert every night. We always sat together in the train. Among other things, he told me that he always set out to dramatize a score. He was by nature an opera conductor and he subjected all music, even symphonic music, to the same treatment. He kept all music living in his mind by linking the music to some sort of human script. He constructed his own stories. Sometimes they seemed a bit far-fetched, but they worked well for him. Every significant phrase was represented by an imaginary dramatic event, and linked to the whole work. This enabled him to imbue all music with dynamic intensity, and the audience never failed to receive his own unique message.

We alternated the Tchaikovsky and the Mendelssohn concerti, and we had a very pleasant routine. In the morning we would travel by train and look through scores. It was on this tour that he guided me through the Bartók *Divertimento for strings*, which he knew better than anyone else, and it is his conception which I shall always keep in mind.

We would usually arrive at our destination by lunchtime. He went to have a rest while I practised. We always had supper together after the concert. He would have his steak *tartare* which he used to prepare himself, and I would have garlic soup, which I have loved ever since I was introduced to it in South America. In Germany, many chefs have never heard of it, but they are usually willing to experiment.

69

In one of the German towns on our tour, after the first movement of the Tchaikovsky, which we had already played half-a-dozen times, he leaned over towards me and – to keep our spirits up – whispered, 'Think of your garlic soup!'

RD: Since the last war so much more music is being heard by so many more people, on radio, television, records and tape. Have you been aware of any changes among concertgoers? Perhaps an increase in knowledge or in attention? A greater readiness to hear a wider range of music?

YM: One of the characteristics of life is that any object or experience is devalued if it comes with little or no personal cost or effort. Every spare moment, every *crevice* of our attention, is being filled and exploited for commercial gain: manufacturers implore us to 'Use our spare five minutes to drink another glass of beer,' and background music says soothingly, 'Listen to me and I will assuage your anxieties.' And if we have nothing positive to concentrate on, we can rely on news of warfare, sorrow, crisis and tragedy, to give us vicarious stimulus.

So much can be seen and heard at the touch of a button. The choice today is enormous. People who want to hear more music, of all periods, now have many wonderful opportunities, unequalled even by professional musicians who seldom have time to educate themselves musically except through their own public engagements.

In music, as in many other aspects of life, there is an imbalance between availability and need. In the days when there were no recordings, no radio, no television, a concert performance was regarded by the audience as a very special privilege. This sense of occasion may be somewhat diminished nowadays, but it is compensated by an increased knowledge of music. Certainly many more young people are coming to concerts than before the war, and they bring an open-minded approach to contemporary music. But I don't think concert audiences have changed in character as dramatically as radio and television audiences have changed in size.

In the theatre and cinema and on television, we see Africans, Indians, people from all over the world, dancing and making music. All races and nations are being brought closer together by the media. But we must be careful that this easy availability does not blunt our urge to travel and meet other people, other cultures, on their own ground.

RD: One aspect of concerts which I imagine is unchanged since the war is the atmosphere of formality. In all your years of concert-giving, what has happened – on the platform or among the audience – to interrupt the formalities?

YM: A concert is a public occasion and people come for a very specific purpose. They have to be passive and yet allow themselves to share in a musical experience. This imposes a certain decorum. Even during the war, when I played for the troops, there was some formality: they all wore uniform of one kind or another, and this gave the audience a corporate identity. Like seasoned concertgoers, they listened quietly and applauded at the end: these are the *minimum* formalities. Another basic element is that the audience should be facing towards the performer.

I can think of several incidents which interrupted the normal concert ritual. One which occurs from time to time – perhaps once every year or two – is a string breaking. Paradoxically this can be a welcome incident, except when it happens towards the end of a long piece of music: I am then in doubt whether to continue from where I left off, or start again from the beginning. For instance, I wouldn't like a string to break when I am playing Bach's D minor *Partita*, which is probably the longest composition in the repertoire for solo violin.

From the very first note of the *Allemande* – to the *Courante*, the *Sarabande*, the *Gigue*, and finally the *Chaconne* – a massive structure is being built. If a string breaks before that structure is complete, the soloist may decide to go back to the beginning. But in various subtle ways the second performance will not be the same. The audience, who came to the recital open-minded, ready for a new experience, have now heard an incomplete and interrupted performance.

The soloist is left with the alternative of starting again somewhere in the middle of the *Partita*, but this is an equally imperfect solution. In a concert, with an orchestra behind you, sharing the attention of the audience, it is somehow more acceptable to begin again in the middle of a work – because in this case the whole edifice is not dependent on a single builder.

Only once has a string broken when I was playing the *Chaconne*: this is the last place I would want it to happen. But my most disastrous experience of this kind was at a concert in the north of England. I had a faulty batch of E strings, and no less than *three* broke during the first movement of the Brahms concerto.

My first diversion from normal concert routine was when I was about eight years old, in San Francisco. After the first movement of the Tchaikovsky I was wiping my brow, but I didn't have a handkerchief. A young lady I particularly liked, who was sitting in the front row with my parents, bounded up on to the platform and presented me with her handkerchief. I *enjoyed* that.

A most dramatic interruption occurred at a recital in Carnegie Hall when Diana and I were listening to David Oistrakh and Richter. They had played one sonata, Beethoven's No. 6 in A major, and were in the middle of the first movement of the Brahms D minor, when a militant Jewish group felt it was their duty to call attention to anti-Semitism in Russia.

One young man got on to the platform, shouting and waving, and completely disrupted the recital. David Oistrakh was clearly very upset, but Richter didn't seem to mind. (I well remember the first time I met Richter. While walking in the garden here in Highgate, I asked him where he had just come from. 'Chicago,' he replied. 'That can be rather a depressing city,' I

In relaxed mood with Maurice Gendron, André Previn and Hephzibah.

suggested. 'Oh no,' he said, '*I love* Chicago. I feel, when I walk down the street, that *anything* could happen!')

Eventually a lumbering policeman was levered on to the platform, a somewhat undignified way for a servant of the law to arrive. The young man was hauled away, and the recital began again. A short while later, another young man, undaunted by the fate of his friend, tried to rush on to the platform. This time the audience were on the alert and they managed to stop him. I saw a policeman nearby, but he was obviously so enchanted by the music that he wasn't keeping guard.

In the interval Diana and I went to the artists' room. Richter was beaming like a naughty cat, but Oistrakh was stretched out on the sofa. He had already had one heart attack by that time, if not two, and his dear wife, Tamara, was very worried about him. Oistrakh said to me: 'Yehudi, were those *your* Jews or *my* Jews?' And I replied: 'Well, David, I am afraid they were *our* Jews!'

RD: You said that the breaking of a violin string can sometimes be a welcome interruption. Would you like to elaborate on that?

YM: The interrupting of the music is most unfortunate, but a broken string dissolves whatever formality there may be between audience and soloist. They feel they have shared an unexpected occurrence with you. They wait patiently until the violin has been restrung, and give you a warm round of applause when you are ready to play again. An unpredictable element has transformed the whole occasion.

RD: Can you recall any other unusual interruptions?

YM: Yes, I remember a concert in Washington DC. On the aisle, in the third or fourth row, a woman was holding a balloon! Sure enough, at a most inappropriate moment during the concerto, the balloon burst. This didn't stop the concert and no one protested. She remained seated, listening intently to the music. She must have been rather dotty, as was confirmed when she came backstage after the concert, still holding the ragged remnants of her balloon.

The memory of another unusual evening has just occurred to me. During the war I gave a concert in Stockton, a city on the edge of the San Joaquin valley, east of San Francisco. The hall seated about 1,500 people. My accompanist and I were playing the slow movement of Enesco's 'Romanian' Sonata when I noticed that the piano and the hall's large chandelier were tilting at odd angles. We continued playing. A hushed groan came from the whole audience. Still we went on playing. Then, twenty seconds later, another earthquake shook the hall and this brought a louder comment from the audience.

There was an unmistakable rise in tension between the first and second tremors; the third caused widespread panic and a primeval moan from the audience, an eerie sound, like the lowing of a herd of cows. People began rushing towards the exit. By this time Enesco's 'Romanian' Sonata had lost all its charm! On the spur of the moment I decided to play the National Anthem. Being wartime, with everybody feeling patriotic, they all stood still: the sound of *The Star-Spangled Banner* proved to be an even stronger force than their panic. They then walked out quietly. After about half an hour most of the audience had returned to their seats and the recital continued – not with the slow movement of the Sonata, because after the earthquakes something more lively was needed to hold their attention. We went straight to the *finale*.

I can remember disturbances of other kinds, such as the grotesque sound when a piano string breaks. And on at least two occasions I have had to stop playing at the beginning of a performance because photographers with flash-guns were busy with their cameras at the very front of the hall.

Once, when I was giving a benefit concert in the lovely church at Lavenham in Suffolk, there was a tremendous roar of planes from a nearby air base, taking part in a NATO exercise. So I stopped and waited until all was quiet again. Any interruption of that kind generates an extra feeling of solidarity between audience and performer.

RD: Then there was the famous occasion when you were delayed in arriving for an Albert Hall concert.

YM: Yes, we had a whole series of mishaps, starting with our take-off from New York. This was in the days of the turbo-prop aeroplane. Three times we went down the runway, and three times the brakes had to be jammed on because of some malfunction. Finally we were asked to go back to the city centre for the night and return the following morning. That evening we went to a concert given by Heifetz, the last time I heard him play. Our plane took off the next day, but an oil leak soon developed and we returned to New York.

On our third try we actually got as far as Shannon Airport in the Irish Republic. There was a dense fog, but it was even denser over London so we were left stranded at eight o'clock in the morning, not having slept. The concert was that evening.

At last, after numerous phone calls and much pleading, we were put on a Boeing 377 Stratocruiser, a plane which had a double-deck fuselage and looked like a hippopotamus. We landed east of London, at Stansted Airport in Essex, in a dense fog, only minutes before the concert was due to begin.

We were whisked out of the plane into a waiting car and driven straight to the Albert Hall. The concert had already begun, Adrian Boult having announced: 'We are waiting for our Hamlet!' The start was delayed for an hour and a half. Sir Adrian then re-arranged the programme and began with a symphony. My arrival, with fingers cold and still dressed in my travelling suit, was greeted with tremendous applause, and I played the Mendelssohn and the Elgar concerti. The ironic part of this story is that Diana and I originally thought we were being over-cautious in allowing three days to get from New York to London.

RD: The theatre is well-known for its superstitions, and a number of them are associated with *Macbeth*. Are there any musical equivalents, such as the *Dead March* from *Saul* or Chopin's *Funeral March* Sonata?

YM: Not that I have ever heard of. Many musicians have their own personal superstitions: something they have to do, touch, hold, or think of, before going on to the platform. I have my own little routine before a concert but no particular superstitions.

The origin of personal superstitions follows a common pattern. Some remembered occurrence precedes an especially successful concert. Instead of attributing the well-received performance to one's own positive attitude or to thorough preparation, the artist endows some trivial aspect of that day with quasi-magical power: if he was wearing a suit with a spot on it, he may deliberately delay having the suit cleaned. And so on. There are an infinite number of variations. On the whole I haven't noticed conductors to be as superstitious as singers and instrumentalists – but they may be.

For thirty years I have carried in my violin case a talisman known as the hand of Fatima, which Diana gave me in Tunis. Fatima, a daughter of Mohammed by his first wife Khadija, is revered by all sections of the Islamic faith. My talisman is a lovely red, embroidered with tiny spangles, and I am very attached to it. I lost it once, for almost a year, but someone found it – I don't know where or how. I was glad to have it back, but while it was lost I continued playing in public without any qualms.

RD: There have been times when you have communicated with your audience through words as well as music. I have in mind your many wartime recitals for the forces; and I heard from a friend that, at a sixtieth-birthday recital in Canada, you and your sister Hephzibah shared some thoughts with the audience about the music you had been playing.

YM: Yes, we did that after one or two of our shorter recitals at universities, where we were invited to have a question-and-answer session with the students. This helped us greatly, through their reactions and responses, to get to know the people we had been playing for.

On occasions not connected with a recital or concert I have also spoken at schools in many parts of the world. I remember a talk in California when I spoke about the dangers of drugs, at a time when this was an especially controversial issue. I referred to drug-taking as a surrender of one's autonomy, and this view was very well received.

During the war, when I played for the forces, I sometimes spoke briefly about the music. There was never a printed programme, so I would announce what I was about to play; and, if this was a piece the audience were unlikely to have heard of, I would say a few words about it. On the whole they were good and responsive audiences.

After a short while I developed a format for these wartime recitals. I usually began with a short brilliant piece, and I found that the most useful one was the *Praeludium and Allegro* of Kreisler. I knew I would catch their attention with that. Then would follow a work of greater length, fifteen to twenty minutes: the Mendelssohn concerto or the first movement of the *Kreutzer* Sonata or a Bach solo, or sometimes even Bartók's first violin and piano sonata, the first or last movement. Then perhaps five or six shorter pieces. The programme would last about an hour. Often I gave three recitals a day.

At first I wondered how to end my recital, because, if I played pieces that had quite a lot of impact, the audience would applaud and keep wanting yet

Opposite: During the war Menuhin travelled to many remote lands bringing music to the troops.

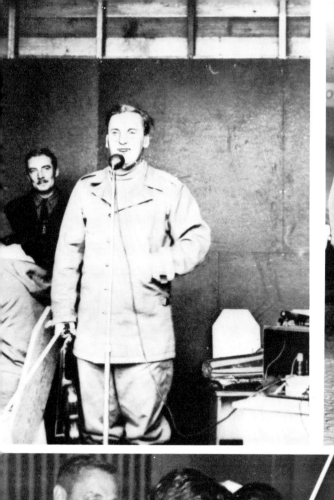

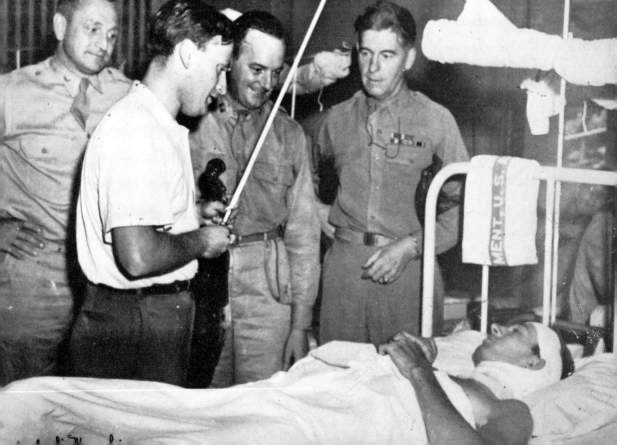

another encore. I soon realized that I would have to prepare for the close by announcing that such-and-such a piece would be my last. It seemed to me that – given the mood of these audiences, and indeed the mood of the entire world – the best possible piece to end with was Schubert's *Ave Maria* which they all adored. It is fascinating, isn't it, how one piece of music can speak so eloquently to man in his desperation?

RD: Reverting to your more formal concert-giving, how do you spend the ten or fifteen minutes during the interval?

YM: Fortunately, my wife comes to most of my concerts. She prepares one of my special hot drinks, to reinforce me for the second half and keep my circulation going and my fingers warm. Before I go back on to the platform she combs my hair.

   I don't like to subject my dearest friends to the crush after a concert, so I sometimes say: 'Do come round in the interval.' But I don't like to spend a lot of time talking during the interval; I'd rather preserve my frame of mind for the rest of the concert.

RD: And then, after the concert?

YM: That depends. If we are in a city which is home to me and where we have many friends – Paris, New York, San Francisco, New Orleans, Chicago, Berlin, Amsterdam, Brussels . . . that is to say, most cities! – the nicest thing is to go back to wherever we are staying, change into comfortable clothes, and be together with a few friends for an hour or two. That I love. What I hate is having to go to an interminable supper starting at one o'clock in the morning. That I regard as an imposition on an artist and I avoid such occasions like the plague – almost always successfully.

   But a quiet meal with my wife and a few close friends – that is a great joy. If the concert is in London, we usually come back here to Highgate and have a light snack. If I am alone on tour, I usually go straight back to the hotel, have a bowl of hot soup and some yoghurt, and then telephone Diana before going to bed.

RD: Do you need to debrief yourself in some way, to bridge the period between total involvement in your performance and going out into the street again?

Menuhin's 50th birthday concert – Sir Adrian Boult, Josef Sivo (leader of the Vienna Philharmonic), Yehudi, Yaltah, Jeremy, Hephzibah.

YM: Diana says that I often look a bit dazed for a few moments immediately after I have been playing; but this reaction vanishes long before I get back home or to the hotel.

RD: One of your violinist colleagues, Pinchas Zukerman, said the other day: 'There is a danger of becoming a musical computer. You reach a certain stage when playing well becomes a matter of physical fitness.' For most of your life, your concert-giving has been programmed years ahead. Has this given you enough personal space?

YM: Bruno Walter used to say to me: 'I'd give anything to be able to hear the great works again for the first time.' I couldn't understand what he was saying. I was only thirteen. I wasn't yet giving concerts day after day, and I had played the great concerti in public no more than five or six times. I gradually came to realize that it would indeed be wonderful to hear the great works as I had first heard them.

And yet I think this is a wish that one can to a certain extent compensate for. We can never recapture the first hour, the first day, of meeting a loved one or of being introduced to a great work of art, but *deep* acquaintance only comes after many years: so much is yielded which was not apparent in the beginning.

The very first time I heard the *Eroica* symphony, the very first time I heard the *St Matthew Passion* – they were outstanding moments in my life. I will never forget them. I was transfixed. I was amazed that music could throb with such power and meaning, such exaltation.

Some of this first encounter has remained. I heard the *Eroica* many times subsequently, conducted by Toscanini and other notable Beethoven inter-preters, and then I looked forward to the time when I would conduct it myself, which I did a year or so ago. Each successive acquaintance brings back something of the first hearing. I am happy to live my life in the friendship of the great works of Beethoven, Bach, Bartók – all the time learning.

RD: Sybil Thorndike said: 'Everything that happens in your life colours your performance.' Yet there are some musicians who don't seem to allow their experience of life, or the deeper side of their personality, to enrich the music they play.

YM: Impediments, blockages, can be of various kinds: physical, mental, emotional. The *mechanical* enters in if you play without full participation of heart and mind. On the other hand, a *technical* approach to music *can* be a quality to be admired. The predictability of a Heifetz performance, down to the most minute inflection, is an example of supreme discipline, and I greatly respect him. But Heifetz is an entirely different artist from my way of being: I want to be absolutely reliable technically, and at the same time I want to *live* each moment.

I liken these different approaches to art to the distinction between an acrobat and a clown. An acrobat or a tightrope walker gives a similar performance each time, whatever their life experience may be. They have to keep correcting their balance within very narrow limits, and they dare not allow their emotions to affect their actions. Not so a clown or a mime artist – they tend, with each passing year, to become deeper, more tender, more touching, more subtle in expressing pathos and joy. The acrobat and the clown are quite different – but they are both part of the same circus.

RD: How do you circumvent the dangers of repetition when on tour with an orchestra, playing the same work several times a week, sometimes even night after night?

YM: For the first three or four concerts there is a rising curve: the performance gets better and better, provided the orchestra is also improving, learning, becoming more cohesive. But after this there is usually a downward curve.

I have discovered, on tours with my own orchestra, how essential it is to rehearse works quite frequently – not necessarily spending a great deal of time on each one, but always coming up with two or three new ideas: 'Let's try this,' or 'We didn't do this quite as well as we might have,' or 'This phrase wasn't quite as well shaped as it might be.' This sort of approach keeps the attention of the orchestra alive, and gives them something new to look forward to at each performance. That is vital if we are playing certain works every day or every other day.

Nothing is more deadening for me, as a conductor on tour, than to have little or no rehearsal time, especially with a big, famous orchestra whose players are very self-confident. In such a case, there may have been two or three weak spots, and I will know they are going to recur. So I begin the fourth, fifth, or even ninth, evening knowing that in a certain part of the score something will happen which I dislike but can't avoid, because we haven't had a chance to correct it. Ideally, we should meet to discuss these points, even if for only half an hour before a concert. This will keep alive my own and the orchestra's interest and anticipation.

RD: We've been talking about performance. I wonder if we might talk about *not* performing – about your sabbatical year.

YM: I would love to speak about it, but I feel a bit of a fraud because, although I am on a sabbatical in the sense that I haven't been booked for any concerts, certainly no paying concerts, all I seem to be doing is play for anniversaries and at memorial services. I am a sitting pigeon here in Highgate, whereas normally I would be on tour and unable to attend these occasions.

I had looked forward so much to my sabbatical, not only in terms of what I *wouldn't* do – that is, I wouldn't travel or give public concerts. Most of this has been avoided. But my sabbatical hasn't yet begun in terms of what I *wanted* to do. True, I have given a few lectures, but that wasn't the purpose of having a year off. I was planning to have a lot of spare time, enabling me to study scores, listen to recordings, and go to the theatre, to the opera, and to concerts. I have done very few of these things. Already eight months have gone and I don't feel that my sabbatical has started. This is a terrible feeling.

Within a few months all the activity begins again. In April I go to the United States, not to give concerts but to publicize my autobiography. I would prefer the book just to appear and not have to bother any more about it. Nonetheless, our many friends say I must come, and the publishers want me to, and I will have an opportunity to visit my parents in California.

I enjoy looking back, recollecting the past, as I am doing with you, but I don't like wasting time on something that is finished. My autobiography is finished. I have said what I wanted to say, but to devote a couple of weeks to signing copies, and talking about the book and my life to journalists and television interviewers, is not at all my idea of time well spent. But I do have, I think, a gift of turning whatever I have to do to good purpose – even if only self-clarification. So when I meet these journalists I probably won't speak about the book at all! Many new things will be happening – in world affairs as well as on the American scene – and I will probably ask them more questions than they ask me! I am sure I will make creative use of that period. In one way I am very greedy – not concerning financial investments, which I am not very adept at, but for a *return on time*. That is very important to me.

In principle, a sabbatical is a very precious time. It breaks the routine of a life's journey. However varied, however exciting and stimulating, my life may be, there are elements of routine. For fifty years I have travelled in trains and aeroplanes, often meeting the same attendants and even the same fellow-travellers. Every trip demands the same routine of gestures: dragging the same suitcases; fumbling for coins to pay the same – or larger! – tips; meeting the same dear smiling ladies at the airport. All of that, at a certain time of life, becomes robot-like. A sabbatical can break a routine such as this, so that next time I am on tour everything will be new again, almost as it was when I first toured and so much looked forward to travelling.

I still enjoy certain aspects of touring: returning to places I know, meeting people I am fond of. As I grow older, I find that meeting people for the first time, in new cities I visit, feels more like routine than meeting old friends year after year. When meeting old friends, close feeling and deep understanding can soon be renewed, even though we may not be able to spend much time together. This is very different from the rather superficial questions of first meetings: 'Where have you been touring these past weeks? What concerts have you given this season? How are the children?' Although by nature I am always interested in people, I was beginning to feel, as I approached sixty, that there was something almost indecent about travelling so much and playing so often: indecent, in the sense that I was going through the motions. I was no longer *reinterpreting* my activities in the same way as I seek to reinterpret a piece of music.

Arriving in Paris or New York doesn't have much of an element of routine.

'When meeting old friends, close feeling and deep understanding can soon be renewed.' Discussing a nuance of interpretation with David Oistrakh.

That is because I love these cities and I love many people who live there. I can't truthfully say I always love New York: sometimes I love it, sometimes I hate it. Nonetheless New York is a place where I know many people, a city that always has a fascination. And I shouldn't be unfair to smaller cities and towns. On my most recent tour of the United States, I went for the first time to Walla Walla, in the north-west, and I found a freshness about many of the prairie and Rocky Mountain towns. But I was interested in a somewhat distant way; I didn't feel the same elation I had as a boy when I used to travel with my father to concerts, before the days of commercial flight.

Travelling by train took up quite a lot of time, and at first I gave only one concert a week. When we arrived at our destination, we would rent a car, drive to a nearby beauty spot, and perhaps park for a while on top of a mountain. Then we would go and visit friends. I would play with the children of the family, and I always hoped they would have a model-railway set!

RD: You spoke the other week of wanting to have a mini-sabbatical each year.

YM: That is what I am planning.

Only three or four months are left of the sabbatical I was so looking forward to. I have gone to the dentist and attended to some other body-maintenance needs which my usual schedule doesn't allow time for. But I had hoped for many visits to my school; many new works studied and prepared; many books read; visits with my wife to the theatre and opera. I have done only one-tenth of one per cent of what I would like to have done.

I am ready for another round of activity, but I hope at a slower pace. For years I have longed to be free in April, May and June. I adore the spring and would love to spend these months quietly in southern Italy or here in England.

Travelling these days is a bore and a chore, because of the pressures at airports, and the crowds, and the delays. The ideal way to reach your plane is by wheelchair, but I can't *yet* allow myself to do that! Arriving, being at your destination, is a delight; getting there is a nuisance.

More and more I enjoy being at home, but I am still young enough to long to be in Paris, New York, Washington DC, San Francisco, Switzerland, Greece, India. I am really looking forward to having years ahead of me – if I am granted those years – to do so many things I long to do.

4

CONDUCTORS

YM: Every musician is unique, but there are certain schools of violin playing just as there are recognizable schools and methods of ballet training. I can trace a kinship among a certain level of conductor – the German *Kapellmeister* or the highly-coached Russian – but most of the conductors I have known have been absolutely individual.

The rôle of the conductor is to re-create a piece of music: contemplate it, make decisions which are his very own, and try to persuade others to think the same way. Other people contribute to the evolution of his approach – he may often consult his orchestral players – but ultimately, like all leaders, he must take not only the final decisions but also responsibility for the result.

With some conductors, to their detriment, the power of the podium is matched by a certain arbitrariness in family and social life. Some conductors, on the other hand, are kind and modest both on and off the platform. Bruno Walter, for example, was one of the most gentle of men.

With me, Toscanini was always very friendly and easy – as I think he was with most of his close friends. It would probably be wrong to say that the iron will he applied to music was as evident when he was away from the concert hall, and yet some aspects of a personality so identified with high standards of performance were bound to permeate his whole attitude to life.

This subject cannot be reduced to a simple formula such as: 'Conductors behave on the podium as they do in daily life.' They don't. I can think of several well-known conductors who are the easiest of people to get along with in a social setting but often become irritable and over-demanding when facing an orchestra.

Conductors are certainly not a uniform breed. When I look back, I can recall so many different personalities. There was Karl Muck, for example, who conducted the Boston Symphony Orchestra at around the time of the First World War, and later the Hamburg Philharmonic. He was a distinguished opera conductor, especially of Wagner. Muck was a tall, erect, commanding figure, a man of few words and no noticeable outward sentiment, his directions to the orchestra always clear, with the minimum of

Toscanini, Hephzibah and Yehudi.

body movement.

Karl Muck was a *very* determined person, formed by the pre-First-World-War Germany which paid such heed to the discipline of school, army, and state, and had a high regard for the dignity and status of a conductor. He was a man of principle and character, a fine musician, upright in every way, in his conducting as in his bearing. I met him in Hamburg when I was about fourteen and played the Beethoven with him. He couldn't have been kinder to me and he liked my playing, but he never allowed himself to unbend.

In those days I asked all the conductors I played with for a photograph. He gave me a picture of himself, signed 'Karl Muck'. I asked if he would perhaps add a dedication. So he took the picture back and very solemnly wrote 'To Yehudi Menuhin' – that was all.

Bruno Walter, by contrast, was much more effusive when signing his photograph – that was *his* way. Walter and Muck were both German, both men of strong character, but they exemplified two completely different ways of being.

I had a great affection for Bruno Walter, as a friend and as a conductor. He was always attentive and courteous to the artists he worked with: his one desire was for the orchestral accompaniment to match the intentions of the soloist.

RD: Neville Cardus called Walter an Apollonian among conductors and Toscanini, a Dionysian.

YM: Toscanini had the temperament of an Italian volcano, but his motive was pure: he was totally dedicated to music. Everyone knew that his tantrums – with orchestras and with himself – were the sparks of a man fired by a great ideal, who *insisted* on music sounding the way he believed it should; and so he was forgiven, quite rightly. Toscanini was a very, very great conductor and I owe him much: for his friendship, for helping me and listening to my playing, for accompanying me with orchestra, and, not least, for the many concerts I attended, always deeply impressed by his interpretations, especially of the German classics – Brahms, Beethoven and Schubert.

Another conductor with a truly Italian temperament was de Sabata. He used to move about so much that I often thought he was in danger of falling off the podium! Nonetheless he was a very fine conductor. The Italians have a rare gift for dramatizing music.

RD: A conductor of a very different temperament is Adrian Boult, with whom you have worked for many years.

YM: Adrian is so very English. His outward quietness belies the intensity of his feelings and of his conducting. He has a gift for concentrating on essentials – of a score and of orchestral texture – and is always striving for perfection of *ensemble*. Everything he does on the podium is achieved with smoothness and flexibility, and an exemplary use of the baton, never clenching it. I know of no other conductor who handles the baton with such ease.

He has a terrific temper, which I have seen only once or twice. On one occasion we were working together on a BBC programme, in the early days of television when the cameras didn't have a zoom lens. At some point in the concerto he suddenly became aware that, in order to get a close-up, the camera had been manipulated to within a couple of inches of his face! He immediately stopped the orchestra and complained with absolute fury. I could well understand his reaction, but I found it rather shattering to see someone like Adrian – who is normally so quiet – lose his temper. Toscanini lost his temper every five minutes: we all expected this and it didn't mean very much. But when Adrian loses his temper, it is like a gigantic upheaval.

Of all the conductors I have known, the most reassuring and inspiring was Georges Enesco. His thoughtfulness and compassion were expressed in every gesture. When Enesco was alongside me on the platform, I knew he was always and in every sense *with* me, giving invaluable support and security.

Another wonderful conductor was Elgar. He just stood in front of the orchestra and they played. The test of a great conductor is the extent to which he can convey his conception with the minimum of anything extraneous, in word or in gesture. Orchestral players knew him, liked him, and loved his music. When we worked together at the famous studio on Abbey Road in London, to record his violin concerto, he scarcely seemed to do anything, and yet, when I listen again to the performance, I know everything was as he wanted it to be.

Malcolm Sargent was a fine conductor, though perhaps not taken as seriously as he deserved to be. He dressed like a gallant gentleman and always had a carnation in his lapel. That suave side of his public image tended to overshadow a first-rate musical talent.

I first met Pierre Monteux in the early 1930s in Paris: together we recorded Paganini's D major concerto, and he used to come and play the viola at our

The young Menuhin with Bruno Walter.

chamber-music evenings in Ville d'Avray. Afterwards we met in San Francisco and in London. He was a benevolent, good-hearted man, rather like a friendly koala bear! As a conductor, Monteux had an easy-going manner, never particularly exacting, but he could always project his overall vision of the music.

RD: Did you ever play with Szell?

YM: No, I was booked for a concert with him in Cleveland about twenty years ago but then I had chicken pox and couldn't travel. He later invited me to conduct the Cleveland Orchestra. By that time he was nearing the end of his life so unfortunately I never saw him again.

I had met Szell in Europe some years previously and heard him give a truly extraordinary account of Beethoven's Ninth Symphony at one of the concerts in Bonn to mark the opening of the new hall. He was a great conductor but one who placed huge burdens on his orchestra, the very opposite of Monteux and Bruno Walter. Szell didn't coax; he demanded, he exacted, he tolerated nothing less than perfection. He showed little compassion for accidental frailties or temporary weaknesses. But his achievement cannot be denied; he *made* the Cleveland Orchestra.

The ideal time to encourage an orchestra to make music is when you follow a martinet. An orchestra is so grateful to play for someone helpful and kind, such as Giulini who – following Fritz Reiner – is now principal guest conductor in Chicago; or Lorin Maazel who has succeeded Szell in Cleveland. Whoever follows a martinet has the twin benefits of the basic discipline left by his predecessor and the relief of the players in the more relaxed atmosphere.

This principle works both ways. An orchestra that has let itself go, not having had a strong enough conductor to hold it together or demand the best it can give, usually welcomes a more authoritarian conductor who will restore a sense of unity and cohesion.

RD: How did Weingartner and Furtwängler convey their authority?

YM: In the Germany of their day – and perhaps to some extent even now – the very fact of being a conductor was quite sufficient to command respect. But their prestige stemmed from more than German respect for rank. They both, in the widest sense, *evoked* music; Weingartner, belonging to a slightly older generation, being rather more traditional in approach.

The only conductors I have known who had to make a show of authority were Reiner and Szell. They produced wonderful results in the concert hall, but in a tense, autocratic way. I admire perfect skill. To be able to train an orchestra so that it plays *fortissimo* when you raise your baton one inch, and *pianissimo* when you raise your baton a quarter of an inch – in itself that is quite an achievement, but it is not my way.

RD: What are your memories of Klemperer?

YM: I first played alongside him in Los Angeles. My main initial impression was of his height. Although he was standing on a very low podium, his head seemed to be at least six feet above mine! Klemperer was a musician of great depth and, towards the end of his life, he joined the select circle of conductors who can stand in front of an orchestra and communicate their intentions with the smallest movement of hands and fingers. Klemperer developed an almost telepathic relationship with the Philharmonia Orchestra: they knew intuitively what he thought and felt, and what he wanted from them.

I have always been fascinated by the way a great musician in later life can raise his playing to a new dimension, and compensate for physical frailty. Enesco, for instance, gave some of his most extraordinary performances when, with back stooped, he seemed scarcely able to play the violin. Miraculously the music emerged with a new purity, transcending human age. I particularly remember the way he conveyed this quality in the 'Geister' Trio of Beethoven, with every note as it was intended to be.

Earlier in life – whether you are singer, conductor, or instrumentalist – you depend on your endowment, your basic talent. Everything must be right: accuracy, tone, overall technical command. In the life of a supreme artist there comes a time when the intention is somehow loosened from outward means of expression: the message comes across on a much thinner thread of materialization. Klemperer was one of the few who have evolved to this stage.

RD: Which younger conductors have impressed you recently?

YM: There are some very gifted young conductors in England, such as David Atherton and Anthony Ridley, and in many other parts of the world, such as Seiji Ozawa and Zubin Mehta. I have known Zubin since he was a boy of ten or eleven, in Bombay. His father, a good violinist, is an excellent trainer of musicians. You can easily see how genes, heritage, and environment have combined in Zubin's favour. His conducting is notable for its ebullience, its tensile strength, and eruptive power.

One of the most brilliant of today's young conductors is Gary Bertini. In

With his wife Diana and Zubin Mehta.

manner and build, he is small, dapper, precise. He has a quick, intelligent mind. He knows his repertoire and has original ideas. Despite his Italian-sounding name he is an Israeli. Whenever the Israel Philharmonic want to play a really difficult contemporary work, they invite Bertini to conduct. He founded the Israel Chamber Orchestra and is now musical director of the Jerusalem Symphony Orchestra: with the influx of some fine Russian-born violinists, and under Bertini's enlightened training, I feel sure it will become one of the finest orchestras in the world.

One of the most gifted young conductors I have ever known is a Finn, Jorma Panula, whose abilities deserve to be much more widely heard and recognized outside Scandinavia. He has a direct way with music and with musicians – reliable, straight, unselfconscious. And he is a truly creative conductor: he doesn't just beat time; he *shapes* music as Celibidache does. Whenever I have played alongside Panula, I have found him a remarkably sensitive accompanist; and I have heard him give an outstanding reading of one of the Nielsen symphonies.

Panula seems to me to be equally adept in all forms of music: operas, symphonies, chamber music, accompanying concerti. He is charming and modest, yet he conducts with no lack of authority or vigour. All that he does – which is considerable within Scandinavia, as composer, teacher, and conductor – *comes* to him. He is not *trying* to make a career. He doesn't exploit life in any way. He is a man and musician of real worth – the very opposite of *publicized* importance.

RD: I wonder if you would like to reminisce about that most characterful of conductors, Sir Thomas Beecham.

YM: Beecham epitomized the English approach to music: he was a most enlightened amateur, in the best meaning of the word 'amateur'. He was exhilarating to make music with because he always saw with a *fresh eye*.

A professional, who works exclusively in one field, often repeats the same kind of activities day after day. The reliability which comes from experience is important, but equally vital is the art of seeing the world – or an old friend or a familiar musical score – always with a fresh eye: this is the special gift of the amateur. He has a whole range of pursuits and pleasures, and so when he returns to his main calling – whether it is painting or music or perhaps one of the sciences – his vision and his enthusiasm are not clouded by dense habit.

All the best musicians combine assurance of technique with the ability to *live* each moment and interpret it afresh. Beecham possessed this double gift to a rare degree. He also had an extraordinary psychological understanding of orchestras: he knew that good things can happen spontaneously during performance which cannot be programmed in advance. Ideally, a conductor should convey his intentions at rehearsal, as clearly as he can, and then leave room for new insight and stimulus to be revealed during the concert. Beecham understood and made use of this process.

English orchestras are remarkably quick and receptive. They don't need – and will not accept – the dull, repetitive drill which certain orchestras I could name are accustomed to. English orchestras have such a fund of initiative and self-reliance that you can *trust* them to translate your expressed wishes into sound without your having to *test* them.

If a conductor can accurately gauge both the music being rehearsed and the musicians he is working with, he will know how to select only those passages which really need a repeat – for the sake of better *ensemble* or so that the players can overcome a particular difficulty. If he shows little trust, wastes their time, and taxes their patience and energy – in an effort to over-insure for a good performance on the night, and in trying to achieve the same results in rehearsal as he wants at the concert – the outcome may prove to be stilted, even ruinous. The more a conductor trusts the orchestra, the more will be his rewards – and theirs – on the night.

The conductor should trust his orchestra as he would a voluntary society, but naturally the players still need to be guided, inspired, held together. No conductor in my experience has had so *light* a touch as Beecham. With very little evidence of drill or use of status, he welded his orchestra into a unit – and yet he *had* authority, much more effectively than a conductor who felt the need to *impose* authority.

The British know much more than most nations about the use of *natural* authority. This has enabled the police to walk the streets unarmed, except for special emergencies. And it has often enabled generations of British high commissioners, in times of crisis, to send a diplomatic letter rather than a gunboat. One of the gifts of the British is understatement: but their understatement carries the full impact of reality and strength. The British excel in being able to distinguish between the overstatement which is mere bluff and the understatement which – as Tom Brown of Rugby first said – means business.

5

CRITICS

RD: Many people imagine that a well-known performer is above the need for personal appreciation of his playing. They suppose that the standards you set for yourself are far higher than the expectations of anyone in the audience.

YM: That is true, in a way. On the other hand, I cannot pretend that I don't appreciate a favourable response from an individual or from a whole audience. For someone to come to me with an unmistakably genuine feeling that he has been moved, has found something new, and that the music has had a deep meaning for him – that is almost indispensable. Even when I am in a recording studio there is a response from the engineers and other members of the technical staff.

When I play alone, I am then both the performer and the responder; but very rarely, in my practice room at home, do I play full out as I would at a concert or recording session. Most of my time alone is spent in careful preparation. I try out certain passages and once in a while I totally abandon myself to the music. But works that I know intimately, and have known ever since I was a child, I try not to deflower too often, so as to reserve something of myself and of the music for the public.

For years, I haven't played the Beethoven concerto right through in my studio. I have worked on many specific parts. I have worked through the score in every way I can think of: thinking afresh about certain passages, checking to see if they match in *tempo*, and ensuring that I can play the music the way I would like to play it. But if my fingers are supple and under control, and if both hands are working well, I don't have to play it to myself from beginning to end. That can wait until the rehearsal.

An artist uses his preparation, his practice, his checks and counter-checks, to smooth and correct any aberration from his path. All these stages are essential to his integrity. A great artist can go beyond these stages, in the moment of performance.

RD: Do you pay any attention to reviews of your concerts?

YM: Mostly I am on tour and leave before the newspapers come on sale or before the reviews are published. I rarely read reviews, but I can't pretend that I never read them.

As a child, I was never shown them. That continued for many years. Then I came to know a few critics; I have never known a great many. In the old days in New York I knew Olin Downes; and Alexander Fried of the *San Francisco Chronicle*, who wrote a review of one of my first-ever concerts, has become almost a member of the family. In England I meet Martin Cooper and other critics at various public occasions when musicians congregate, and as fellow-judges of music competitions. Joan Chissell of *The Times* always writes with warmth and kindness about my school. Edward Greenfield is a very sensitive and knowledgeable critic for whom I have great respect. I came to know Felix Aprahamian and to value his qualities, critical and human, when I joined his championship of Alexandra Palace, where, encouraged by him, I conducted Handel's *Messiah*.

I look upon critics as honest, hard-working people who do a very difficult job. They have to try to be open, alert and aware, night after night. They have to listen to the same works over and over: this must be wearing for them unless they hear an outstanding performance, or unless they are in the mood for a particular work, composer, or period. So much depends not only on the performance but on one's own receptivity.

Sometimes when I go to a concert, every note *means* something to me. Other times I go and don't seem able to *participate* in the music – perhaps because it is being played less well than it can be; or the programme may contain heavy, lush, romantic music, whereas what I feel like hearing that evening is something elegant, clean and spare. Another day I might love to revel in Tchaikovsky or Sibelius, but instead I am served a spartan, dry-as-dust musicological meal.

Music criticism is highly disciplined and exacting work. Critics have to try to be detached from their own inclinations, give a fair account of what they have heard, and assess the music, the performance, and the occasion. It is no wonder that they seldom do justice to all three. They often concentrate on the music itself or on the performance; they rarely convey a sense of occasion. That is something for the most part outside their ken – except for someone as enlightened as Neville Cardus. This is a pity, because an audience congregates for an *occasion*, and the collective feeling that binds the audience to the performance is not the least element in a public concert.

Critics are sometimes schoolmasterish. It may be their duty to mention an

out-of-tune note or a slip of the finger here and there, but such details should be given in their full context; often they are totally irrelevant.

My own view is that generally critics are well able to assess a performance, but when they try to explain the whys and wherefores about the success or failure of a performance, setting themselves up as amateur psychoanalysts, they are almost always wrong – and that is a very good thing! It is probably just as well that critics are limited to what their ears report, and don't know what goes on in the mind and heart of a performer.

The public often wish to be educated, they want to be guided in their future choice, and critics do their share in this important work. They also contribute to the BBC's Radio Three, which I regard as one of Britain's most important single educational systems. But there is so much more to the musical life of a city than its major concerts and opera productions. A lot is going on in the schools and academies, with new attitudes to music and to teaching; new chamber groups are being formed; composers are developing, experimenting. I would like to see a broadening of commentary on music.

Having said that, I confess to a certain ambivalence about the whole subject of criticism. In a way it is a pity that music has always to be commented upon. For centuries, folk music was played and tribal dances danced without there being any review the next morning! And concerts have taken place during weeks-long newspaper strikes, without observable impoverishment to musical life.

There is something about our analytical and didactic era which clamours to see a record in print of everything that happens. I don't pretend to know the reason for this compulsion, but I believe it to be a threat to all that is spontaneous and creative in art.

RD: In my lifetime, that is to say since the last war, the critic with the broadest outlook and the finest literary style was undoubtedly Neville Cardus. When did you first meet him?

YM: I was extremely fond of Neville Cardus. I first met him in Australia in 1936. He was a critic who never lost sight of the occasion, nor of the *intention* of the artist. He was anything but a schoolmaster critic. He read into an interpretation all that the artist wanted to say, even if one didn't fully succeed in saying it. Cardus *understood*.

His perception of potential reminds me of the first time I played Bartók's solo sonata, in Carnegie Hall in 1944. Bartók had completed it only a few months earlier. However well I may have played the sonata then, I realized I still had a long way to go before I could play it as I wanted to. Several times in the past few years I have wished that Bartók could hear the sonata as I can now play it. But I feel sure he realized what my intentions were. Perhaps he *did* hear the music, thirty and more years ago, as I can play it today.

Neville Cardus had the same quality: an intuitive perception which was so encouraging to artists. To feel that someone can understand what you are striving towards is an enormous help. Cardus was an outstanding critic and a charming friend – to me and to so many others.

RD: One of the interesting things about Neville Cardus is that he had only a few singing lessons early in his life, and never played an instrument. Perhaps his ability to enter into the workshop, as it were, of the composer and the performer owed something to his not being burdened by the finer technicalities of music.

YM: Exactly. He responded in the way a naturally informed concertgoer does. He never lost the *innocent ear* because to the very end of his life he *loved* music.

I sometimes wonder how many experienced critics still love music. I am reminded of the conductor at a rehearsal who looked at his glum-faced first violinist and asked: 'What is troubling you? Is your wife ill?' 'No,' came the reply. 'Is your child ill?' 'No.' 'Are you sick?' 'No.' 'Well then, what's the matter?' 'I *hate* music.'

RD: To what extent are critics interpreting for the general public the rapidly evolving language of music?

YM: The critics in London are doing a very good job. I can't keep up-to-date with all that they write, but what I do read from time to time convinces me that most of them come to hear a new work having studied the score and already formed some opinions about it. You may question if that is necessarily a good thing. With some music, it might be better for critics to hear the first performance before studying the score: I am speaking of music that is relatively easy to appreciate at a first hearing.

RD: Which composers do you have in mind?

With Wilhelm Furtwängler: 'He evoked music.'

YM: The music of Malcolm Arnold, for example. He is such a genial, good-natured man, and a most fluent composer. He wrote for me a concerto for two violins and string orchestra which I have played quite often with one or other of my violinist colleagues. Much of the music of Malcolm Williamson also makes a strong first impression.

With works by composers such as these, I would prefer a critic to come to the concert without having looked at the score. As soon as you begin to analyse and dissect, you lose a precious amount of spontaneity. A critic who comes unprepared might write more enthusiastically about the music.

But there are other works that need repeated hearing and deep study. Some of them require several years of acquaintance before being accepted by the critics, and perhaps a few more years until they are accepted by the public – especially if the works are in a new musical dialect or language.

There was a period when critics tended to frown on any music that was too light, too simple, too 'old-fashioned': music that had understandable harmonies was considered *passé*; any work that was euphonious – the music of Frank Martin, for example – was considered scarcely worth listening to.

In the last few years I have noticed a return of acceptance for romantic music. During the high period of the dodecaphonic [twelve-note] school, some of the Bruckner and Mahler symphonies were regarded as old-fashioned; but now all over the world, we have conductors and orchestras, audiences and critics, revelling in these symphonies, with their big thick sounds. These days, works are more likely to be assessed according to their intrinsic merit.

Fashions come and go. Some critics are scholastic and austere, and recoil from any music that is romantic or sensual. At one time there was a fashion against beautiful sound. A few well-known violinists had tried too hard for beauty of tone, often at the expense of the music's intellectual content. They would twist a work all over the place – like an unscrupulous Italian tenor – to produce their applause-winning effects. In time, these artists were considered vulgar and they gave way to a new breed of violinists who hardly vibrated, rejected swooping *portamenti*, and played only the written-down grace notes. Everything was played strictly in *tempo* and was both aesthetically pleasing and musicologically correct. And that style was widely accepted.

As with fashions in women's clothes, fashions in music now come one after another like a continuously revolving kaleidoscope. Every soloist follows his own muse and is listened to on his own merits: there is no longer a bias towards one style or against another. A beautiful tone is acknowledged as a beautiful tone.

For years, critics would comment on every aspect of a performance – but with one exception. They never seemed to mention quality of sound. To have done so at that time would have been considered *infra dig*. And yet a violinist's sound, his tone quality, is one of the most important aspects of violin playing. Today, I am glad to report, critics are willing to concede a beautiful sound.

We have also had changing fashions in recording technique. After the war there was a cult for minimum reverberation. The studios were so arranged as

With Sir William Walton, studying the score of his viola concerto.

to produce a very focused sound, and this was supposed to be pure music. Then everyone went to the other extreme and recorded in the most resonant churches, because the public wouldn't accept the trend towards austerity.

Thank heavens for a public prepared to assert its own heartfelt needs, wanting beauty of sound, and preferring a candle on a restaurant table to neon lighting overhead. The public wants *atmosphere* in these days of such unabashed ordinariness, when seemingly everything is available, and yet so little has its own bloom: a flower is seen by some as only so many petals and is just as acceptable dried or made of plastic. The scent of a flower; the siting of flowers in a garden; the opening, blossoming, and eventual fading, of a flower – all these are ignored.

Sound was once subjected to the same synthetic approach: sound was just sound; the quality of sound, the lingering of sound, the resonance, didn't matter at all. Then, when that failed, and records were not selling well, even though they were being produced by the most advanced recording techniques, the engineers began to add artificial resonance, and finally they settled for Kingsway Hall which has a naturally beautiful resonance.

Fashions can be dangerous: a deliberate, wilful, intellectual, theory can become a one-sided creed or dogma. We live in an age which is forever synthesizing intrinsic qualities: giving us an injection of vitamin B12 instead of liver and fish; condensed versions instead of the books themselves; encounter groups instead of the ebb and flow of daily living. Vitamin injections, condensed versions of books, and encounter groups, all have their place, but we must not become over-reliant on them.

A leading record company once issued records containing the most popular passages from the great symphonies. People could listen to all of Beethoven's nine symphonies on one LP and imagine they really knew these works. Music, of all the fine arts, is an exercise, a sculpture, in the art of time; unfortunately some people are so pressed for time that they violate music by assuming they can encapsulate it. But time and music refuse to be compressed. Can you imagine going on to a dance floor and being told by the bandmaster, 'We will play only the first eight bars of the "Blue Danube" waltz?' The activity of dancing requires a certain area of floor space and a certain amount of time. As soon as you take into account the human body and physical activity, you give music its full importance. Music cannot be compressed in time any more than the process of digestion can.

6

COMPOSITION OF MUSIC, AND THE PURPOSE OF THE ARTS

RD: High among composers you have most affinity with are Bach and Beethoven.

YM: Yes. Beethoven, Bach, Brahms, Schumann, Schubert, and all the way through to the modern school. I feel very close to Bartók, more than to Schoenberg, though I like much of Webern. I also feel a great affinity for Johann Strauss, Offenbach, and Bizet: I should love to conduct *Carmen*.

I have, I think, a fairly wide range, partly because I have come to know so many different countries and cultures: I have many Hungarian friends; Romania I loved, and India; when I was young I lived in France, England, Switzerland.

I listened the other day to a couple of Delius concerti which I recorded with the Royal Philharmonic: the violin concerto and the double concerto for violin and cello, incredibly rich and romantic music, and Paul Tortelier played beautifully. I am ashamed that it has taken me the better part of a lifetime to become acquainted with these two concerti.

RD: What do you feel about British music of this century?

YM: I regard it as music which has kept a balance between the pressures of modernization and the good old-fashioned virtues of counterpoint, of singable music, and of music that is somewhat related harmonically. I see 20th-century British music as a direct inheritor of the traditions of Purcell and John Dowland.

I never could go along with the extreme abstractions of the neo-Viennese school of Schoenberg and Alban Berg. In their time it was, I suppose, necessary for composition to be approached in a theoretical way, but this has never appealed to the English mind, which is more intuitive, pragmatic, whole. The English trust nature and this, I sincerely pray, will prevent them from ever adopting an artificial dogma or becoming slaves to a theory. The English will find solutions which are sensible and humane. This is why I have

With Sir Michael Tippett.

enormously enjoyed my years in London and continue to do so.

Lennox Berkeley; 'Sandy' Goehr, an experimenter whose music is eminently playable; Richard Rodney Bennett; Malcolm Williamson, who was born in Australia but now lives in England; and of course Walton, Benjamin Britten, and Michael Tippett – they have all written music which is individual, in the best sense, and free of any one theory or style.

RD: You were a close friend of Britten.

YM: Yes, ever since we first met towards the end of the war. I was about to leave for Germany to play for displaced persons and survivors of concentration camps. He begged me to take him as accompanist. Those days with Ben, bringing to the victims of human madness the solace of music, rekindled and clarified our life-mission as artists.

We took a large suitcase of scores, including most of the well-known, and also some of the less hackneyed, violin repertoire. Ben brought the same care and zest to the brilliant or sentimental shorter pieces as he did to sonatas and concerti.

Fortunately for me, when the Aldeburgh Festival was established a year or so later I was able to continue my musical partnership with Ben. It was a mark of his generosity and musical integrity that he invited to Aldeburgh many other composers, of all ages, and included in his programmes the widest range of periods and styles, whether or not he was particularly sympathetic to them. And he encouraged me – by his presence as performer as well as by his advice and experience – to start a festival of my own in the town of Gstaad in Switzerland.

When you think of his genial works for children – *Let's Make an Opera!*, *The Young Person's Guide to the Orchestra* and *Noye's Fludde* – you realize that, although he had no children of his own, all the world's children were his. Throughout his life Ben maintained a youthful vision. At the same time, he knew that sacred inner torture which is the hallmark of all great creative minds, for he possessed genius much larger than the human frame can comfortably contain.

RD: What you have been saying about Britten's genius reminds me of one of John Ruskin's aphorisms on art: 'The best part of every great work is always inexplicable: it is good because it is good.' Would you agree that, ultimately, mystery is inherent in all greatness, whether greatness of a human being or greatness of a work of art?

YM: Yes. Greatness in music, for example, resides in what the composer wanted – and was inspired – to tell us; in his aesthetic conception of form, style, and content; and in his craftsmanship. The interaction of these factors is infinitely subtle and complex. If we receive something of the deeper message of the music, we don't know what to ascribe it to; we can only continue to try to collaborate, and enter the mind and soul of the composer and his music.

To someone who hasn't been able to collaborate in this way, a composer's music may even appear banal. Although I feel rather cynical and over-sophisticated to say so, I find much of Bruckner's music quite banal; but if you try to share the working of his mind and seek to understand what he

Menuhin with Sir Lennox Berkeley.

wanted to convey – as, by now, thousands upon thousands of concertgoers have – he speaks of something very real.

There is an indefinable element which *transforms*, which makes a work of art beautiful and, in its own way, perfect. We find this, for example, in architecture. Diana, when she looks at the front of a building, asks herself what mood it conveys, and likens it to the expression on a human face: some buildings smile; others glower.

The façade of a Georgian building is good-natured and tolerant, avoiding excess of ornamentation, avoiding eccentricity and wilfulness and ambition for power and grandiose gestures. A Georgian building makes no effort to impress, but this is not a sign of meekness: the building gains strength from its perfectly natural proportions. For me, Georgian architecture is the most livable of styles, the most reposeful and wholesome. But *imitation* Georgian architecture, despite seeming to have all the essential hallmarks of the style, lacks that indefinable element which distinguishes the real from the artificial.

I should like to return to my wife's apt analogy with faces. Some faces have pleasant expressions; other faces have disagreeable expressions. Furthermore, pleasant and disagreeable expressions occur at different times on the same face. Only an artist can catch that subtle alteration of line which depicts the *moment* of transition in a facial expression from joy to pathos; or which marks the difference between the real and the imitative in architecture.

I have never taken the time to analyse the differences between Mozart and the music of his contemporaries. But there are scholars who have studied this, and I wonder what they have discovered? There is something unique about a great composer's work, even though he may be creating within an accepted style or framework. He constantly reveals his own individual ways of thinking: in his use of the language of music, in his shaping of phrases, and in his ability to spring a musical surprise on the listener.

But the crucial difference between good art and great art – whether in literature, or music, or painting, or sculpture – is to be found in the quality of the original inspiration. The *inspiration* of genius is more deeply experienced, has greater unity, and is more far-seeing. The *workmanship* of genius has a natural sense of proportion; speaks of human elegance and understanding; and deeply touches our own life, thoughts, and dreams.

There is music which *attempts* to be elegant but isn't, just as there are people who attempt things which don't suit them. You can go into a room and find it sympathetic; you can go into another room and find it revolting.

Taste is a result of both subjective and objective factors: subjective and individual, depending on a person's temperament, age, and cultural and familial background; objective, depending on the degree of subtlety in his *awakening* to the beautiful.

RD: Do you regard chamber music – and especially the string quartet – as the highest form of musical activity?

YM: Yes, I do. The independence and interdependence of each line; the subtlety of inflection and of the emotions expressed; the restraint, the economy of instrumental resources – a quartet can convey so much more than a huge orchestra with a battery of brass, producing an ear-splitting volume of sound, each composer trying to outdo the other in decibel-strength.

Where do we go from here? Our civilization has a fatal preoccupation with centralization and control, and with size. So much is out of proportion with the human scale: distance is no longer measured in distances we can walk or run; heights are no longer the heights we can climb; vehicle size exceeds by tons what man alone or animal-and-cart can haul. Excess size creates inflexibility.

RD: The glory of the string quartet is derived not only from its compactness but from the number four being symbolic of wholeness.

YM: Yes. A string quartet covers more or less the range and divisions of the human voice, male and female. It can express the deepest and most sensitive of human emotions. It can speak of eternal truths. A high degree of constant mutual adaptation is needed because there is no piano to set the pitch. The potential volume ranges from the infinitely soft to sound which can fill a room or a concert hall. The range of tone quality is vast.

An orchestral score requires much doubling of parts, with regiments of instrumentalists playing the same note. Also, a quasi-military discipline is needed: each section has to use the same bowing, and so forth. This reduces the importance of each individual member of an orchestra. I am not decrying the great works written for orchestra, but I am in no doubt that the string quartet, in which each player has total responsibility for his part, is a more

Overleaf: 'Music for music's sake' – the Menuhin–Kentner–Cassado trio.

subtle and evolved form of communication.

One of the joys of the string quartet is that it can be played by amateurs, enabling them to become acquainted with some of the finest music ever written. The quartet belongs essentially to the home. It is music for music's sake, and for the sake of those who play, and the few who may be listening. For all these reasons, the string quartet is the purest form of music.

RD: What is your attitude towards electronic music?

YM: I remember attending a concert of electronic music introduced by Leopold Stokowski in New York in the mid-Forties. There were no less than three tape machines – of an exotic-looking breed – on the platform. This was music history in the making, one of the first eruptions of electronics in a public performance.

Stokowski was always in the vanguard of musical movements. He was a man of extraordinary vision: 'This is the music of the future,' he said to me. He was then in his late fifties but he still had wide-ranging interests, a sense of new discovery, sureness of judgement, and a flexibility in mind and body, all of which a much younger man would have envied. It is heartening to see older artists remain open-minded and adventurous.

In personal relationships, Stokowski tended to hide his youthful exuberance and great fund of enthusiasm behind a mask; a mask that was solemn almost to the point of affectation. His dignified manner seemed controlled and self-conscious. I never saw him free, jovial, abandoned.

Since then, I have heard a little more of this music, but not enough to form a clear impression of how an image or sensation is translated into electronic form. Nor do I know to what extent electronic music now has its own grammar.

Electronic music opens up enormously wide possibilities, offering an infinity of sounds and intervals; you can, as it were, add to them, subtract from them, multiply and divide them. My first reservation, therefore, stems from this very richness, this unlimited wealth of opportunity.

In any of the arts we usually have specific limitations. And these limitations are precisely what gives the art its character, its quality, its economy, its *pointedness*, and also – if we can understand the idiom – its capacity to communicate.

Now, when we can do *anything* we want to with sound, we must find a unifying field principle. Einstein was searching for a field principle that would account for all phenomena, inorganic as well as organic; and one of my favourite philosophers, Brunner, later postulated just such a principle, bringing together animism and monism. According to Brunner, we make a false dichotomy between organic and inorganic: he saw all matter as being, to some degree, in motion, animated, and conscious of its motion.

In the past, a composer didn't have to create his notes from infinity – the notes already had a certain pitch – but with electronic music the composer has to master entirely new elements of pitch, notation, and presentation to the public.

I am not arguing merely as a dispossessed manual labourer on behalf of his union! I am thinking aloud in musical terms about what electronic music can represent and what its possibilities and responsibilities are.

My second major reservation about electronic music is that the rôle of the interpreter, and his ability to establish *living* contact with an audience, is lessened. Sound changes all the time and only exists *in* time: sound is a living penetration of our ears, our body, our psyche, and as such must be subject to minute variations of pitch, intensity, and so forth. Electronically, a perfect note could be devised; but it would appeal only to the senses, not to the emotions.

Electronic music may well be suited to become the music of the spheres. I was rather embarrassed – when I saw on television the first moon landing – to hear the American national anthem. Somehow it didn't seem to fit the occasion, because the moon landing was both forward-looking and backward-looking, an achievement of advanced technology and a reminder of ancient disciplines. An astronaut must be able to live alone, or with a few other people, for weeks at a time: to face isolation as well as the ever-present risk of death, he needs a mental balance characteristic of a monk or a yogi.

At the top of Everest, you have come to the highest point on earth; you are still man. But when an astronaut walks on the moon he is in a way cut off from the earth, although in constant communication. He has to keep warm and protected and be given oxygen. Our technology, our electronics, our space vehicles and equipment, are all adaptable to conditions on the moon; it is the human body which is at a real disadvantage there. Perhaps electronic music can represent this temporarily disembodied state.

RD: Is there any music in the established repertoire that could equally well represent this state of being?

YM: You could put forward an equally good case for some of Schubert's songs; they might remind the astronaut of the essential integration of body, mind, and heart. On the other hand, they could cause him to feel a despairing nostalgia for all that he had left behind and might never see again. For that reason, the most apt music might be electronic music specifically composed to give the astronaut a sense of space, a sense of infinity, without reminding him that he is a husband, a father, an American.

An essential characteristic of music of the spheres is that it should be contemplative in mood: music that raised your blood pressure, or inspired you to dance up and down, and then use up more than your quota of oxygen, would be anti-social. This is the reverse of our current values, at least in the west. Here we are considered social when we are jovial and back-slapping. People like Bartók – who was highly economical of language, who never uttered a word that wasn't absolutely essential – are usually called unsociable. I only hope that any planet found to be habitable has enough oxygen for laughter.

I have yet to be convinced that electronic music can convey tenderness; but it may well be able to simulate the sound of rustling leaves or the murmur of a stream. The fresh, sweet, gurgling sound of water is an ever-recurring feature in Schubert's songs. Throughout history, the sound of water has been one of nature's most captivating sounds for mankind. The oldest recorded civilizations used water in the most ingenious ways, practical as well as decorative: everything from air-conditioning to the highest aesthetic use, such as the sight and sound, outside a public room, of the gentle flow of water bearing rose petals.

Electronic music offers welcome possibilities for experimentation. I would like to see electronic kits for children: a tape machine with various means of modifying sound, and also a pre-recorded tape containing a whole variety of basic sounds – some that have clear associations with nature; others that are non-specific. A child of nine or ten would then be able to create his own composition.

I would like to see other kinds of kits, containing African tribal music for example, so that a child could become acquainted with music from all parts of the world and from many different forms of society.

RD: What are your feelings about pop music?

YM: Pop music, when it originates spontaneously, in the back streets of

Liverpool, as with the Beatles, or on the wrong side of the tracks in a city in California – this I am all for.

Pop music degenerates when it becomes heavily commercialized, has little musical content, and appeals only in a compulsive, hypnotic way, feeding the desire of a large group of people to blot out everyday thoughts and cares. The senses are then horribly battered, and for a time the audience are no longer balanced, moderate human beings. That is what I fear and that is what frightened me when I went to hear a world-famous pop group.

One day I received a letter from their manager, saying he would like to give me 100 tickets – for the opening performance of a new London season – to sell for the benefit of my school. This sounded like a most generous offer, and so my secretary, Eleanor Hope, who has great initiative, put a small advertisement in a newspaper, giving the telephone number of a friend of hers, who soon received dozens of calls. We sold the tickets at colossal prices and made a lot of money for the school.

I felt I had a certain obligation to go and hear the group, and their manager invited me to join him. He turned out to be a very distinguished man from a West-European aristocratic family of high lineage. He has done much to improve the group's financial affairs. He loathes their music – but not the money it generates!

I was appalled. The music, if it can be called that, was a kind of torture, calculated to dominate the senses. I was determined to resist, in order to remain true to myself. The only other course would have been to say: 'All right, I give in.' The sheer volume of sound was overwhelming and it was no consolation to learn afterwards that the amplification system had been faulty. I left before the end because I was feeling so ill at ease.

I don't like to surrender my self-composure: I like to feel that I am in possession of myself and all my faculties. On the other hand, I surrender willingly to Bach, Beethoven, or Schubert. I will *prostrate* myself in front of them or any great work of art or a temple or a tree or a person I love – because, in so doing, I become *more* myself.

But I couldn't in any way participate in this cheap, noisy, contrived, depersonalizing entertainment, so-called. Thousands of pounds had been spent on the lighting, the sets, the presentation; the group wore clothes covered with sequins and rhinestones which reflected the bright light. From my point of view, the musical content was virtually non-existent.

I looked at some of the young people in the audience. If I had told them what I was feeling, they might have castigated me and said I didn't understand their pleasure, their needs, their identification with the music and the pop group. What they might not have realized was that they were in a condition in which they could be led.

When I left, the mood of the audience was on the verge of hysteria. Having lived during the time of the Nuremberg rallies, I have a horror of mobs. I was disturbed by this enormous audience of young people, imitating every gesture of the group on stage, their senses and emotions being abused and taunted to produce commercial gain. I feared that, having lost all sense of proportion, the audience could be dominated, coerced. What terrified me was the compulsion towards unanimity.

The most *un*unanimous audience is the Israeli: some will applaud, some decide not to, and others look quizzical, dubious. By the end, the artist usually has them all applauding, but only after convincing each one separately.

At the other extreme are the German audiences, who are no less discerning but react as a disciplined unit. Often, at the end of a work, they will keep silent for a moment before applauding: I find this framing of music in silence very moving. It represents a certain *pudeur*, a feeling of embarrassment at intruding with noise upon music.

On the other hand, we know where collective discipline can lead when it is wrongly guided, when people have an uncritical trust in organization, authority and efficiency for its own sake. This is passivity; humility in an audience is something quite different. Humility can be felt in a church service, for example, when the congregation has been deeply moved by a combination of music, preaching, incense, and the atmosphere and history of the building itself.

But I was aware of no humility in the mood of the vast audience which had come to hear the pop group, and we know how easily and how fatally the borderline to unconscious forces can be crossed. I felt the *proximity* of that borderline, and I loathed and feared it.

I am not condemning; I am warning.

RD: Perhaps Ruskin can put us back on course; for, of all critics, none has been so concerned with the true purpose and ethics of art. He once wrote – and it seems very apposite to what you have been saying – 'The end of Art is as serious as that of other beautiful things – of the blue sky, and the green grass, and the clouds, and the dew. They are either useless, or they are of much deeper function than giving amusement.' How do you see the rôle of art and the artist in society?

YM: When I think of art, I think of a range of activity which has been part of humankind since man's very beginnings. Art is *inseparable* from life, and I don't believe any artist is justified in supposing that he, or what he does or creates, is of excessive importance. An artist is a servant.

Art is also inseparable from nature. Man and animals are united by the same urge (what the Germans call *Drang*) for beauty. No human invention or art, visual or aural, is without its counterpart in the animal world. Why should the peacock have such beautiful feathers, and not only have them but know how to display them? Here surely was the original inspiration for the fan.

The same basic impulse which inspires man to re-create beauty, in colour and shape and sound, and to decorate a room or his own body – that same impulse is manifest in the evanescent grace of the lyrebird, with its melodious song, ornate feathers, and plumes which are used to form a canopy over its head.

Human-created art begins with self-dialogue, with self-consciousness in the widest sense, and ends with the communication of what we see of ourselves and others, and of what they see of themselves and of us. An artist's self-dialogue is a constant adjusting, correcting, re-balancing, of elements within himself. The very basis of life is to develop imbalances – often unconsciously – which we then correct. Perfect balance with no separation, would be no life at all; continuous imbalance would offer no means of resolution.

We need to cultivate self-awareness – that is to say, knowing when we are off balance – and then moderately and subtly deal with the imbalance, without going off balance in the process of correcting – as when we try to balance a walking-stick on the tip of a finger. If the stick goes beyond a certain angle at a certain speed, we cannot restore it to balance, and it falls.

Our basic yearning for balance is a kind of nostalgia for a state of perfect equilibrium: happiness is not only a feeling or condition we aim for in the future, it is a conception of balance that is alive deep within us from our experience of the womb. How to reconcile this internally-held ideal of perfect balance with the flux of everyday activity is the basic problem of human life. Life itself is a constant state of movement. The question we need to answer – with the help of the artist, the priest, the philosopher, the tightrope walker – is how to maintain balance in an environment of constant movement.

A gyroscope is an example of perfect balance, but it is individualistic, creating – according to its speed – its own balance. Our human balance-requirements are infinitely more complicated because we need to be in balance not only with and within ourselves but also with other people and our changing surroundings. Many of our fellow-men have a partly-conscious, partly-unconscious inclination to push us off balance and reduce our value and importance. This perverse use of power is a very strong force: someone who isn't balanced, who isn't self-aware, will try, by every trick of word and gesture, to make himself seem superior to others. Instead of seeking contentment within, he tries to overcome his uncertainty by abusing, exploiting, manipulating others.

We all have a need to be at one with ourselves, in order to withstand the onslaught of unbalancing factors, of a thousand and one kinds, from inside and outside: ill-health, discomfort, frustration, and so forth, as well as interaction with other people, who themselves are at the mercy of unbalancing factors. It is precisely at this point of universal human need that art can make its most influential contribution.

A good example of this particular function of art is the use of masks by primitive cultures. Their masks represent aspects of life, including spirits, evil elements, which inhabit all human beings. By depicting these spirits, by giving them form, by shifting them from inside to outside, their subversive power is diminished. Art can then be seen to have a two-fold purpose: it is a reflection of the artist himself, and it is an avenue of communication along which other people can discover more about themselves.

Art can be created by the high-minded as well as by people enslaved by drug addiction. The art of Bach, Handel, Shakespeare, Goethe, is balanced and wholesome; but much of the art of our day is created by people with a disturbed equilibrium. This has far-reaching implications for our whole civilization.

I don't make major distinctions between the greatest art of the last few hundred years – such as the art of Michelangelo and Leonardo da Vinci – and the art of the caveman or the art of the potter. These days we should have a more *crafty* approach to art!

Folk music is mid-way between an art and a craft: the whole tribe dances and participates, and is part of the creative process. At the same time, a tribe will still have, and give recognition to, its best musicians, its outstanding potter and sculptor. Art, in all societies, has its hierarchy.

Art is indivisible from the facts of existence and survival, from the need for communication, for sublimation, and symbolization. I agree with Ruskin that art has a deeper purpose than giving amusement, and I have been speaking with you about the more serious aspects of art; but I also love the lighter side. And the lighter side of art is just as important: an evening of Strauss waltzes or of folk music is *essential*.

I adore gipsy music. What would gipsies be without their music? It is inconceivable. They would no longer *be*.

RD: You were speaking earlier about Germany. I should like to read you a few lines from Bonhoeffer's *Letters and Papers from Prison*: 'Music . . . will dissolve your perplexities and purify your character and emotions, and in time of anxiety and sorrow will help you to keep going a ground bass of joy.' This leads me to wonder if perhaps music is the most *consoling* of the arts.

YM: Music can penetrate all one's defences. The combination of music and an especially poignant occasion can be unbelievably potent. When I heard the Amadeus play at the funeral I recently told you about, the slow movement of Schubert's *Quintet with two cellos* took on an entirely new meaning for me. Until hearing it in those circumstances and those surroundings, I had only skimmed the capacity of that music to *move* and to *mean*: I now realize that it can both give out and absorb any amount, any depth, of emotion.

As a child, I felt music very intensely. Music was everything to me. I used to cry myself to sleep night after night with the sole companionship of certain melodies. Although I then had hardly any life experience, I must have felt an inkling of what the Germans call *Weltschmerz*: an awareness that I mustn't cry or feel anguish only for myself.

As you grow older and are exposed to life, music becomes imbued with all that you have experienced. To experience life and to translate that experience into music is the task of both the composer and the performer. So many people are destined to experience life without having an opportunity of translating it, except vicariously through listening to music or enjoying one of the other arts. This is the only form of vicarious experience that I can accept as having a positive function.

We all have joys and tragedies, ecstasies and struggles, but we may not have enough experience of life to draw the full measure of emotional depth or rational analysis or philosophical meaning from what has happened to us. We need elucidation, and so we go to the great creative artists whom we can trust, such as Bach or Beethoven or Shakespeare. The experience of the most

evolved people – whether artists or religious leaders or people from any profession or background – opens our eyes, broadens and matures us, and unlocks our repressed feelings, giving them shape, sound, form, and meaning. A great work of art *re-presents* human beings to themselves.

Music, unlike the visual arts, lives in time. The music of Bach or Beethoven captures our vibrations, compels co-living. I am prepared, without reservation, to live through Beethoven and his depth of experience, but what I cannot accept is the almost total subservience that cheap entertainment demands. I want to be informed, enlightened, enhanced, by art; I am not willing to be presented with the crudest sensations – fear, cruelty, bizarre behaviour.

When evaluating art and artists, we need some understanding of the subject of hero-making and hero-breaking. All societies – whether communist or western democratic – are pyramid-shaped, although there are wide differences in gradient from one type of society to another. People are torn between reverence for those at the top of the pyramid, and frustration at not being able to get to the top themselves. This ambivalence leads us to put people on a pedestal and then want to drag them down.

Britain, in its wisdom, has a Royal family at the head of the community, and ensures that Royalty preserves a neutral, and thus a protected, rôle. Infinitely more vulnerable is a film star or pop idol. An idol is a false god, and many pop idols are so ordinary in their personal life, so easy to imitate, so subject to common desires – drug addiction, alcohol, greed – that people can quickly identify with them – and equally quickly dethrone them. This speed of building up and knocking down reflects the pace of modern life; it also gives the idol-maker an inflated sense of power.

Only by enquiring into the nature, function, and creation of the human idol and the hero can we learn to distinguish between those artists who possess a *natural* authority and will have a long-lasting and beneficial influence on mankind, and those artists whose life-purpose and work are ephemeral.

Opposite: Prince Charles visits the Yehudi Menuhin school in 1970.

7

TEACHER AND PUPIL

RD: What are the characteristics of the good teacher and the apt pupil?

YM: Some less able teachers have produced wonderful results – with apt pupils; some very competent teachers have not always produced good results. I try as well as I can to understand the particular difficulties of each student; and I try to make my suggestions as clear as possible, without assuming that I know every answer. The teacher who is rigid, who believes there is only one approach, who imposes it and wants unquestioning compliance – such a teacher misses a great deal of the enrichment that comes *from* the student.

Some methodical teachers have been successful despite keeping to a rigid approach. In ballet, for instance, there have been ruthless teachers who insisted on the following of every instruction, even the most trivial. Russian teachers – of all subjects – are often exacting, and impose strict routines and methods. They have produced many fine instrumentalists and ballet dancers. Among tens of thousands of students, there are bound to be those who somehow manage to survive years of tension and pressure, and are still able to preserve elements of the flight and imagination which prompted them in the very beginning. Of those who survive, a given number emerge from their studies with superb command and technique, and go on to reach the heights.

However, I believe this has been achieved at great human cost: these strict methods haven't yielded as much as was possible from those who have *not* made the grade. Our system, at its most enlightened, develops the ability, the initiative and the imagination of those who are not strong enough to endure a tough, rigid, highly-structured style of teaching.

Only a truly gifted teacher can be ruthless and exacting and at the same time be successful; a mediocre teacher who is ruthless usually has a most destructive influence. An inspired teacher can be harsh up to a point, but even he will cause terrible pain and break many a young heart if he doesn't show compassion and understanding for each pupil.

On the other hand, the indulgent teacher, who is forever saying, 'Very good . . . I know you have done your best . . . You are really very promising,' who seldom corrects, and doesn't present an ideal of what the highest standards are – he is doing just as much disservice to the student as an over-strict teacher does.

I meet a great many teachers these days who are over-anxious to please their students. They try to win them over by handing out lollipops, rather as some churches do in America by inviting reluctant parishioners to come to a turkey dinner – *after* the service!

In teaching, this is a total mistake. If the child wants to learn, you don't have to adopt be-good-and-I-will-reward-you methods. A teacher should be content to work with the natural ingredients of the relationship: his own inspiration to teach; the child's desire to learn; and the wonder and joy *inherent* in music.

Teaching requires a whole gamut of qualities: sensitivity, discretion, determination, and an understanding of why a particular attempt by the student does or doesn't work. Often a teacher will say, 'Listen – this is the way it should be done,' without giving the child any idea of *how* it can be done. Some teachers are spoiled – by their best pupils – into assuming that every child can do the same. Other teachers, once their methods and routines are established, are unwilling to rethink, dissect, and re-analyse them, for the *specific* needs of *each* child. Teaching, at its best, calls for a great deal of self-analysis, not only of yourself, your personality, but also of your playing: so as to be able to show a child *exactly* how to achieve improved style and form.

The capacity to learn is much greater, and is a more mysterious power, than many teachers realize. They assume that a child learns a kind of musical alphabet from A to Z, in a logical sequence. But a talented child is learning all the time, at many levels and in many settings: in the hours of formal teaching and everywhere else. All that he hears and sees and feels and tries to apply enriches a personal yeast, as it were, which ferments and expands and creates its own expression, its own way of playing music.

The teacher offers guidance here and there, but the *primary* factor, the driving force, in your relationship and work together is the student's own commitment and desire to learn. Teaching is like sailing: the wind and the sails give the boat its motion; your rôle is to steer and guide.

The teacher must never forget that he isn't making all the important moves and contributions; he isn't in control. He has before him a child with a living motive element. The child will do much of his own finding and discovery, once he has learned how to experiment.

Violin playing and teaching are a matter of sensation, inner and outer. You cannot communicate a ready-made sensation; a sensation can only grow from within the individual. The most a violin teacher can do is try to give a clear conception of what it feels like to play absolutely in tune; how playing middle-of-the-note corresponds to your image, your dream, of perfect sound; what a wonderful feeling of total freedom and balance you experience when you are playing well.

The next stage is to try and find out, in a spirit of mutual discovery, what is obstructing the ideal. Is it the stance? Is it the angle of one of the arms? Is the bow being clutched in a stiff, anxious way? Any incorrect use of any part of the body prevents achievement of the basic principle – and that is the floating sense of being in *balance in motion.*

The sensation of balance in motion is known by the diver and the tightrope walker, but is missing completely from most teaching of the violin. The conceptions and methods of the unenlightened teacher are rigid and fragmentary: 'You stand like this . . . You hold the violin like that . . . You hold the bow . . .' And so on and so forth. Whereas in truth you don't *hold* anything; you *balance* everything.

The good teacher – of violin playing or of virtually any subject – is one who communicates the sense of being carried along, and encourages you at the same time to be constantly correcting – your posture, your progress – without falling. And the good teacher conveys not only a sense of being carried along, but also of giving yourself, abandoning yourself, as much as possible.

I regard as unenlightened the idea that you can rely on one position or posture or method for ever, saying, 'This is the way it should be, and this is the way it will remain.' You cannot perform or create or paint or sculpture with that attitude. Ideally, you must always feel that you are *in* balance *in* motion.

RD: I am sure you will share my appreciation of a Sufi saying I came across the other day: 'There are no teachers. We are all learners.'

YM: That is absolutely right. I often learn as much from teaching as the pupil learns from me. Teaching is a constantly reciprocal relationship. The idea that a pupil is a passive recipient, a container waiting to be filled by the teacher's knowledge and instruction – all this is nonsense. Teaching is a *living* relationship, of give and take, of *mutual* learning.

The wonderful benefit for the teacher is that you have to *formulate* what you would like to communicate. An older musician, and one who plays well, may not feel any impetus to re-create either his own style of playing or his approach to teaching. Too many teachers are so formed in their way of playing that all they can do is perform in front of the pupil. That is not sufficient.

You have to be able to demonstrate by your own playing, but you also have to show *how* you are achieving certain effects, and that takes much effort and self-examination. I am discovering more all the time while trying to formulate, in an exact and lucid statement, how to hold the violin; how to move the fingers; how to check that the various parts of the hands and arms are flexible, free, and in balance; how to co-ordinate and unify all these factors.

These are the fundamentals. When you come to questions of interpretation, they are in a way both easier and harder to answer than the basic things I have been speaking of: easier, because correcting takes place in the ear and via one's whole attention; harder, because you are dealing with elusive matters – nonetheless, they are more amenable to clear description than you might imagine. For example, if certain notes are more important, they require a little more length or warmth or expression.

It is a most helpful discipline to be able to play all the notes with equal value, but, beyond that stage of attainment, you have to *shape* the phrase. You have to know: where the high point is, and where the phrase begins to wane; which notes represent the continuity, and which are only embellishments; what overall impression or atmosphere you are trying to communicate – serenity, struggle, grandeur, wit, or elegance. In addition, and permeating the musical material, there is an element of energy: smooth or jagged and impatient. This needs to be felt and communicated in order to impart the right flow, the right texture, the right impulse.

The undulation of time is both subjective and objective, and, as you play, it is possible to sense the ebb and flow, inner and outer. Music is an art of time, and playing is a relationship – shaping time and being shaped by time.

RD: A friend of mine said the other day – almost casually but with much wisdom – 'The best teacher is the one who himself has had to struggle to learn.'

YM: I am sure that is true. I imagine that whatever contribution I can make to teaching derives from having had to rethink and re-create my technique: it was quite adequate, if you listen to the early recordings, but it was the *intuitive* technique of a talented child. At that time I knew the *feeling* of playing beautifully. This was essential because it later enabled me to re-find that experience on another, more conscious, level. As it turned out, my re-learning took quite a long while, but I think it would have been impossible had I not known for years what it feels like to play well.

However well I may have played as a child, my analytic mind – during my re-learning period – wasn't satisfied until I knew *how* it happened. There are other people who go through life without having, as it were, to take the watch apart and then reassemble it. The watch works and this is all that matters to them.

What I have been able to learn from my own experience is, I hope, enough to set a student on the right path. With some children, a few lessons can change their whole way of playing.

A teacher doesn't lead his student through every aspect from A to Z. Rather, he sets him on a course, gives him a new conception of where he is going and what to look for. With a talented violinist, this may be all that is necessary – starting a process. Each new discovery along the way is a satisfying one, so a dedicated student, once started, will keep going, keep looking, keep searching. Teaching, in essence, is a matter of launching a student on the search, in the right direction.

RD: When you recall your own teachers, what are the first and best qualities you remember?

YM: Ignition, first of all . . . the basic kindling. One is grateful for every stage of teaching – technical, interpretative – but the first thing you need is ignition. I remember one of the few times I have ever been on the back of a horse. I was in California with a friend from childhood days. He wasn't much better than I, and we had been given two safe and trusted and very old horses. They wouldn't budge. My friend turned to me and asked: 'Where is the self-starter?'

Ignition cannot happen unless the student is already committed to a way of thought, of life, of values.

RD: What you have just said reminds me of the eastern saying: 'When the student is ready, the teacher comes.'

YM: That is so true. Ignition doesn't happen in a vacuum.

Ignition is followed by *inspiration*. In my case, the lifetime's devotion to music of Georges Enesco and Louis Persinger – loving music, serving it, believing in it, seeking to understand it more deeply – was communicated through their *attitude*.

Even as a child, I had reliable instincts about the right choice of teachers. I didn't choose my teachers just for their technical ability. They were pedagogues and at the same time much more than pedagogues: they were musicians, composers, performers, who were regularly appearing on the concert platform. Louis Persinger was concertmaster of the San Francisco Symphony Orchestra. He studied with Ysaÿe, was a soloist, and formed his own quartet. Enesco was a composer, violinist, conductor, pianist, caricaturist, punster, and linguist. In addition to his native Romanian, he spoke the most elegant English, French, German, and, I think, Russian.

Bartók was never my teacher, but I would have given anything to have studied for a couple of years with him. He was due to come – in what turned out to be the last summer of his life – and spend a while with me in California. Unfortunately his health prevented him, and I have a letter saying how sad he was that he couldn't travel all that way. Three months with Bartók, that summer in California, would have been one of the greatest gifts a musician could dream of.

My conception of a teacher – based on my very fortunate experience as a student – is the very opposite of a dull driller who goes through the same books and the same routine – year in, year out – and says the same things to each successive year's class of children. On the other hand, I recognize that we need the kind of teacher who knows his job, who can not only illustrate but also explain, who can correct minutely, and pinpoint specific causes of malfunction.

A child above the age of eight or nine needs more than just a good example. He needs a firmly-based understanding of music and of himself: he needs to become aware of the sequence of thought that prompts a given sequence of action. Thus there is an important function and justification for a pedagogue such as Carl Flesch or Leopold Auer. They were not in the front rank of interpreters, they were not composers or conductors, and they were certainly not fiery Romanians, like Enesco, with an understanding of the gipsy and at the same time a deep, living knowledge of the greatest works of music and literature, classical and modern. They were eminent pedagogues, and made their own special contribution.

I have just such a teacher at my school, Felix Andrievsky. He was assistant to a great Russian teacher, Yankilevich, who died recently. Conforming to the Russian pattern – of man and wife being in the same profession – Andrievsky's wife is a pianist. I could quote many other examples: Leonid Kogan is married to a violinist; Rostropovitch to a singer; and

Menuhin with Rostropovitch in Paris, 1974.

Rozhdestvensky to a pianist. This is one way in which a society can consolidate and concentrate its means of advance. But this extreme specialization – musicians seldom meet engineers; doctors never meet astronomers – works to the detriment of the broader development of the people.

I now feel that the teaching at my school should rely mainly on professional musicians, most of whom are still performing in public, together with a few specialized pedagogues who work according to an established routine. These pedagogues follow the methods of their tradition. Their teaching may seem less improvised than that of others, but they have not been dulled by their calling; they are, like Andrievsky, lively, inspirational, and dedicated.

RD: It seems to me that one of the main faults of much of our education is the lack of development of imagination and intuition.

YM: There is a *yearning*, throughout the western world, for the intuitive. Sadly, this yearning can be so strong as to take all sorts of monstrous forms: the desire to *abandon* oneself as an escape from regimentation, legal and administrative. The individual in man longs to be seen and accepted as more than worker number 41,043 fulfilling one narrow function.

The reaction among the younger generations takes various forms: defying and flaunting the law; abandoning themselves to the most powerful and primitive urges – violence or promiscuity or alcohol or drugs; wanting to rebel against almost everything and everyone.

Every generation rebels: no doubt, this *has* to be. As a way of declaring your independence, you turn your back upon the recent past – the people, the events, the way of life – and then eventually, and at first a little reluctantly, you retrace your steps.

I was talking with my wife yesterday about parents and children. She said: 'Why is it that they never seem to give us trust and credit for our intentions? We try never to intrude. We try not to impose rigid rules. We are always here when they need help.' I replied: 'They are good children, as good as any. But at a certain age they have to go away and in a sense look on us as adversaries – even if we have been the kindest of parents.'

RD: *Especially* if you have been the kindest of parents.

YM: Yes, I am sure you are right.

Children in their teens are longing to go out into the world. They become ever more aware of the limitations of their parents. They decide to cut the emotional umbilical cord. Their turning away may have more than a touch of aggression: 'I'll have little or nothing more to do with you. Whatever you tell me I will subject to the closest scrutiny. I will be as suspicious of what you say as I am of everything outside home. But the outside world hasn't hurt me yet, so I'll give it the benefit of the doubt. In fact I'll give it *more* benefit of the doubt than I give you and all that I have known up till now.'

When the widest possible divergence has occurred, the slow reuniting begins – provided the parents live long enough; and have been prepared to wait patiently, and not take retaliatory action which they might later regret. If only we can learn to accept that in life, in every human being, in every relationship, there are rhythms and cycles and patterns that we cannot avoid.

Our physiology, our psyche, everything about us, is subject to forces we must learn to use and guide, without allowing them to destroy us. I compare this to the wonderful Red Indian oarsmen who can ride the rapids in a canoe. We would almost certainly perish in those rapids, but the Indian has learned how to negotiate them.

Adults still have much to learn about being able to accept and understand young people, and moderate them. The propulsion of society depends on a certain amount of undifferentiated power, which has to be guided. A car engine converts the natural explosion of gasoline into the rotary movement of the wheels. If the explosion occurred in the open air, you would have no driving power at all. The explosion is confined and made to work in one particular and useful direction.

RD: What you have been saying about the learning process within a family – the parents' need for patience and a sense of timing; and finding the right stance at each stage of an ever-changing relationship – all this has its counterpart in teaching.

YM: Yes, the dynamics between teacher and student are similar. There comes a time when the student turns his back on the teacher. His playing cannot have the necessary security, autonomy, self-faith, or communicative power, until he believes his interpretation is his *own*.

As a conductor at rehearsal, what I try to do is *release* the interpretation which the assembled musicians would ideally like to play. I seek to achieve a result which is *natural*, from the point of view, simultaneously, of composer, audience and performers.

My working hypothesis is: 'This is my view of the best interpretation, but if a George Malcolm says: "According to my musicological research, this phrase was not played in that way," then I will listen to both versions and not decide until the theoretical, the practical and the intuitive are satisfied.' I don't care whether the chosen version is mine or somebody else's, so long as it is right – as right as it can be, according to our collective feeling and knowledge. Ideally, the instinctive response at a final rehearsal should be: 'That is the way we have always *wanted* to be able to play this music.'

There is a potential inspirational quality among the players – to the very back desk – of every orchestra. The more blighted and blunted their lives have been, musically speaking, the more grateful and happier they are if you awaken that element of inspiration. This is the best and ultimate purpose of conducting: not only to lead them and keep them together, not only to make their performance easier and simpler, but also to guide them so that they can play as they have always *longed* to play. Then you get a resilient, exuberant response – something more than they or you had hoped for.

RD: One of the recurring themes of our recent conversations has been the transfer of authority from outside to inside: parent to child, teacher to pupil, conductor to orchestral player. I believe that the ultimate aim and final stage of teaching is the introjection of the teacher, the taking in of him as a permanent internal figure. It seems clear to me that your teacher, Enesco, has become part of your living experience. He is still alive, in you and through you.

YM: Yes, he is, although I am so much less of a musician than he was – in any measurable terms. I don't know a fraction of the repertoire that he did. I don't have his memory for music. I don't have his gift for composition or his ability to play the piano; nor will I ever match up to his violin playing or his intellectual and spiritual qualities.

Nonetheless, there is something of the character and core of Enesco which is *very much* with me. I recognize this in certain ways I play and interpret; in certain attitudes to people and to life; perhaps in a certain chivalry, one of his

Opposite: 1962: With that great teacher, Nadia Boulanger, in the city of Bath whose annual music festival Yehudi Menuhin directed for many years.

supreme qualities; and also in the romantic streak in my personality. In all these ways I was greatly influenced by Enesco, and continue to be.

As I look back with you now, I can see that – although they didn't meet often, for it was my father who took me to lessons – there were many similarities between Enesco's values and those of my mother. Enesco, a man in the gallant, chivalrous and patriotic European traditions of Jan Masaryk and Paderewski, reinforced the Russian-bred influence and values of my mother, one of the most spirited and determined of women.

RD: When you are teaching, how easily does imagery – by way of illustration – come to you?

YM: I love to use imagery. I am not sure that my mind is as fruitful or as agile as I would like, but whenever I can, whenever a tangible image comes to me, I use it. I try to compare a particular emotion or passage in a piece of music with some aspect of life, from sports and games to the characteristics of an animal's movement. I do believe there isn't a single thought or concept, however abstract, that cannot be rendered simple enough for a child to grasp.

I am not always successful – sometimes an image eludes me – but aspects of violin playing, such as weight, speed, pressure, balance, and economy of motion, suggest many parallels. Provided my suggestions are natural, and conform to the laws of gravity and the anatomy of the body, I am convinced that perfectly clear examples can be found which illustrate tangibly and unambiguously, and sometimes forcefully, to whoever is trying to learn, the point I am trying to make.

RD: How much imagery did Persinger and Enesco use in your lessons with them?

YM: In the *dolce* passage in which the violin is accompanied by *pizzicato* strings, at the very end of the first movement of the Beethoven concerto, after the cadenza, Persinger wrote 'Worship' – just that. All my teachers had a deep *reverence* for music, a sense of service. The great conductors I have worked with, such as Walter and Toscanini, conveyed that same feeling; and so do the staff and children at my school. But I rarely find this quality today among the confident young technicians I hear in music competitions.

Enesco used imagery occasionally: not often about technical matters; more usually about moods and emotions. On my violin part of the Beethoven, at the point in the first movement, before the second big *tutti*, where the violin plays very softly as it rises higher and higher, Enesco wrote 'Contained dignity'. Those two words implied such a lot to me: I took them to mean an atmosphere of serenity, independent of anything else in the world, continuing in a quiet, gentle, unhurried way.

Enesco was so versatile. He used to sit at the piano and accompany me in concerti and sonatas. He didn't use very many words; he spoke to me through the music. He did say it would be useful for me to read more about the lives of composers, and he advised my father to take me to Salzburg to learn more about Mozart. Enesco said: 'There isn't a note or syllable in his music – whether for instruments or the voice – that isn't a word and a gesture. You can only understand Mozart by going to his operas.' So my father promptly and very wisely took me to Salzburg that summer. We were there for a couple of weeks and went to the opera every night. That was a most wonderful period, and it left its mark.

Although for the most part Enesco let music speak for itself, the words he did use were always illuminating. Of the second subject of the first movement of the Elgar concerto, he said: 'That is very English.' At the time I had little idea of what he meant, but now I can see exactly. Enesco was speaking of a kind of adult innocence, sublime and yet earthy, which is a very English quality. I am always intrigued that the French – probably the *least* innocent people in the world – tend to imagine the English are far more sophisticated, more devilish and more shrewd, than they are.

From my own observations, the British mind and the French mind function in very different ways. The French are often completely demoralized when what has been uncalculated turns out to be more accurate, more successful, than what was planned by rational means. The great British achievements have been due to an extraordinary combination of intuition, courage, faith, and innocence. The British seem to win without wanting to!

The French, nonplussed, take refuge in assuming that the British are being cunning; but the innocence of the British is not a false mask. On reflection, there may have been just a tinge of irony in what Enesco said about that passage in the Elgar; but he was a good and straightforward man, never sarcastic, and I know for sure that he adored the English.

As a family, when we used to cross the Atlantic, we usually travelled on French or Italian ships, such as the *Rex* and the *Conte di Savoia*. But not Enesco. He said: 'I always travel on an English line. They know more about

With Epstein, 1945.

the sea than anyone else.' Although he had never spent much time in England, Enesco understood with remarkable clarity the country and the qualities of its people.

RD: What is your attitude towards the master class?

YM: That depends on the composition of the class – who is leading it, and the students' own stage of development – and also on the prevailing mood among those taking part.

Enesco used to conduct master classes with remarkable facility. These were held in Paris at the house of Yvonne Astruc. I only managed to get to one or two of his classes.

A master class is a cross between a lecture – an exposition with illustrations – and specific attention given to individual students. A master class can be a valuable way of communicating interpretative ideas, and can also help to resolve problems of technique.

Several times, after spending a half-hour or an hour with a group of violinists, I have received most encouraging letters saying: 'My hour with you made a tremendous difference. I now play with far greater fluency.' This form of teaching is like the scattering of seed. One method is to choose the right soil, dig a furrow, and plant each seed carefully. Another method is to take a handful of seed and scatter it: some will fall on fertile ground.

A master class has a similar element of chance. Often you have never met the group of students before; and, after a short series of classes, you may never see them again. They raise whatever problems they are currently struggling with, and during the hour you say whatever comes to you, at any given moment: some students will respond; others may not. There is no set sequence.

The master class can complement – but not supplant – regular forms of teaching. Being an addition to normal routine, a master class can give children that spice, that new angle of thought, which they might not otherwise receive. Sometimes they respond as if the blinkers were removed; all of a sudden they take a wider view.

One value of a master class is that the children are introduced, however briefly, to a new teacher. Influence does not necessarily correspond to length of time, even in friendship. You can meet some people every day and never feel close to them; you can meet others only once every few years, and yet a deep relationship continues between you. For a child, who is with the same teacher week after week, an entirely different person to talk to about music can provide a real stimulus.

RD: You give the impression of enjoying your teaching more and more. Are there any qualities about children when they are learning that you marvel at even more than you did in the past? For example, their ability to concentrate?

YM: Oh yes, I never cease to remind myself that I may be underestimating children and their many capacities. Even though I was fairly advanced as a violinist at a young age, and even though I listen to children at my school who play beautifully at the age of eleven or twelve, I constantly discover that children have much more potential than we credit them with. All we have to do is help to release what is already in them, and put them on the right road. We need to be able to talk *their* language, and translate our own thoughts, which may be abstruse or philosophical, into precise and tangible illustrations.

RD: There is a subject you touched on earlier about which I should like to hear more – that is the rôle of the teacher-performer. It seems to me useful – even vital – for a teacher to be himself working on pieces of music for performance.

YM: This is something I want to establish at my school. The concept of the teacher who also performs is a very good one. There are many parallels: for instance, in some hospitals the leading consultants are also teachers. The musical profession is in danger because of a split into two methods: an academic form of instruction and instruction by example.

In general, I believe that the best teaching is done by those who have the fire and the experience of performing; but I have known some remarkable violin teachers who have seldom been on the concert platform as soloists. One of the most wonderful teachers in this category – although he did make a few concert tours early in his career – was Demetrius Dounis, a Greek–American, whose published exercises are among the best and most ingenious ever devised for the violin. I greatly admire his work. I probably could have met him in New York and shall for ever regret that I didn't. Many of my colleagues went to him and he helped them enormously.

The nature of life and of mankind is always more complicated than we imagine, and no aspect can be expressed in one sentence, one formula. That is why, having made a statement, I usually want to articulate the opposite, and then try to reconcile the two. Thus, the reverse of what I have been saying about the value of the teacher-performer is that I have known many

Opposite: Menuhin with Pierre Monteux in Bath Abbey: 'He could always project his overall vision of the music.'

instrumentalists, including some very fine ones, who couldn't teach.

RD: Why is that?

YM: Someone who has been accustomed to playing well all his life, who has had great talent from childhood onwards, may rely mainly on instinct and intuition. He may never have had to analyse and eradicate defects of technique, and so has never discovered intellectually the basic principles.

One day, when I was about eight or nine, I was speaking to a wonderful violinist, Michel Piastro, who was concertmaster of the San Francisco Symphony Orchestra after Persinger, and then became concertmaster of the New York Philharmonic under Toscanini. I had no true *staccato* and still haven't, even though I have played and recorded the *Hora Staccato* by Heifetz. Possibly, with the help of a teacher such as Yankilevich or Auer or Flesch, I might have mastered it. Anyway, as a young child, I said to Piastro: 'You have a beautiful *staccato*. How do you do it?' He was a man full of goodwill. He would have told me if he could, but he couldn't. He said, 'I do this: I do that', but he gave no real explanation of method. Piastro was born with a beautiful *staccato*.

Each one of us has a special knack for *something*, and some reveal their gift very early in life. This gift is a product of the genes: an albatross, despite its size, is able to fly; a particular human being's nervous system or metabolism or reaction-time works in such a way that he is able to excel in some aspect of life. Whether or not he makes full use of his gift is another question.

These days *staccato* is taught quite well. Among the violinists who played at the Carl Flesch Competition recently were a couple with the most incredible *staccato*, played with such speed and clarity that I could hardly believe it. Neither of them won first prize, because unfortunately they didn't have very much more than some aspects of brilliant technique.

I wonder if they will ever become teachers? A performer isn't automatically also a teacher, not at all. A player of modest ability who has had to analyse and struggle to achieve technique, and is able to explain and illustrate in words as well as with the instrument, may turn out to be one of the best teachers.

At my school we have a teacher, Eluned Chapple, who works in conjunction with the professors and supervises the children's practice. She spends half an hour a week with each of the violin and viola players, and makes an important contribution to the teaching. She did a certain amount of chamber-music playing early in her career, but little solo work.

RD: You spoke a moment ago about the ability of an albatross to fly. It is interesting to look at teaching in the light of what we are discovering about the animal world.

YM: Yes, a fascinating subject. For example, would a fledgling hatched in the absence of its parents, and in the absence of their example, learn to fly as well as they can? I would have to ask an ornithologist. An experiment such as this has almost certainly been done, and would tell us to what extent flying is instinctive, an inherited ability, and to what extent it is learned by example. There are certain insects which never see their parents. The parents die several hours before their offspring are born, and thus there is no possibility of teaching. The young have to climb a particular type of shrub, they have to reach a particular type of leaf – all this is in the genes.

If we relate that to human life, we discover how much of man's climbing, as it were, is ingrained in the ethos of the time. Astronauts have been in the imagination of man for hundreds of years: walking on the moon is a very old conception. What *is* new is the technology which has made space-travel possible.

I wonder if we shall ever be able to distinguish with precision between teaching by example – life's formation of a human being – and the heritage and endowment a child already has at birth. During the war many men who served in the US Navy with skill, imagination and courage came from the mid-west. Most of them had probably never been near the sea before, which shows how versatile a human being can be. And today, some of the best and most penetrating playing and conducting of our European classical repertoire comes from musicians who were born and brought up in the far east. Conversely, one of the worst performances I have ever heard of Enesco's 'Romanian' Sonata was given by two Romanians who had just won first prize in a music competition in their own capital city, Bucharest.

The mode of learning goes through different stages: first, there is the inherited; then example; gradually, learning by example gives way to a more deliberate, more self-chosen learning. The analytical part of the mind then begins to play a bigger rôle, in questioning and integrating.

All through life, we have to contend with habit. The total organism, body and psyche, needs a yardstick whereby it can recognize and reject what is harmful, what is stultifying. Too much of our life is ruled by *unrecognized* habit. We have to live with ourselves as well as with others, and many of us therefore ignore what we don't like about ourselves.

And yet this very element, seemingly unwelcome, may be essential to the artist, the composer, the performer. Prejudice is the spice of life. Too much – like too much pepper – is not good, but a little prejudice, a little bias, contributes to your identity, your personal style.

Bias is a burden you have to carry, and it disturbs the equilibrium. The urge to achieve and maintain a certain balance – which is a lifelong quest – provides the very heartbeat and circulation of an artist's work. If the bias is too strong then it will impair your playing, your survival, and cause damage to yourself and to others. But a *slight* bias gives your bowing and your *vibrato* a recognizable, personal touch. It may be faulty or frail, but it has its own little edge, sharp or soft, which is not unsympathetic, because it enables you to leave your own imprint on an interpretation. That amount of bias – or prejudice, spice, imperfection, whatever you want to call it – is part of life itself.

If we ask ourselves what it is that a teacher can contribute, or what we can do that animals cannot, or what distinguishes our era from past eras, it is the ability to *synthesize*, to find common factors. Without that, our science and our philosophy would be nowhere.

Yesterday, while preparing for a talk on BBC television, I was considering what Europe and the west has to offer to the rest of the world. I came to the conclusion that Europe's special gift is the ability to synthesize and harmonize. Whereas the rest of the world's music is mainly monodic in origin and tradition, harmony is a European innovation.

Harmony allows many voices to sing together, with the minimum of friction and the maximum of consonant sound, and with many possibilities for the alternation of tension and resolution. Music in Africa, and in many other parts of the world where people in a community sing together, is usually against a held note, or else in unison or in octaves. The special quality of harmony is that the voices can move independently but within given limits – *if* they want to cohabit on the same page of music!

Europe is the repository of so many great and powerful human streams. They each remained very much themselves and at the same time had to learn to live together. They had their commercial exchange; and they finally adopted one language, Latin. They adopted one religion, Christianity, which divided into Roman Catholic, Orthodox and Protestant – and is now seeking

On a visit to Léopold Senghor, President of Senegal, in 1977.

Menuhin, seen here with Edward Heath, was the first musician to be awarded a degree by the Sorbonne.

reunion. A musical style evolved which, although different from country to country, was nonetheless recognizably European. The ruling families had their individual territory and responsibilities, but were inter-related, from one end of the continent to the other. They had wars, with one nation – the Romans or the Scandinavians, the French or the Germans – trying to impose its will on the others. Finally, having at last realized that, with all these unique and strong voices, there is no possibility of one dominating all the others, they got together in Brussels and formed the European Community. They decided that the only way to co-exist was to harmonize, synthesize, find common denominators between diverse peoples and cultures, diverse aims and needs.

Harmony, in its widest sense, can be found in many forms: in the four-voice choir, in contrast to the snake charmer playing his flute; in democracy, the opposite of tyranny; in the synthesizing capacity of our evolved societies, in contrast to the one voice of an indigenous culture.

Thus the true and overriding mission of our western education is to *humanize* our capacity – in so many aspects of life – for synthesis, for blending, for bringing together.

8

YEHUDI MENUHIN'S SCHOOL

RD: So far we have been talking about teaching in general. Now may I ask you to tell me about your school?

YM: One of the chief characteristics of the school is its integrated nature, both in terms of the wide range of subjects and activities – from music to the natural sciences, from cricket to rehearsing an end-of-term play – and the unity of all members of the community: the headmaster and his wife, the teaching and domestic staff, and the children themselves. Everyone seems to be aware of this unity, as if they were all part of a musical or dramatic work, each person contributing to the whole.

All over the world thousands of communes have sprung up in a spontaneous attempt to create harmonious existence between people. Inevitably, this requires effort, awareness, and dedication. People sometimes imagine that group harmony consists merely of putting pieces of a jigsaw into the right place – careful selection of the members, sensible financial arrangements – and that then all will be complete and self-propelling.

The main difference, as I see it, between a community and the jigsaw-puzzle metaphor is that a community is living, growing, changing, and must constantly *reassess* itself, *reappraise* its conceptions and commitments, *refresh* its emotional well-being, and ultimately find creative satisfaction for the group and for the individual.

Our highest satisfaction is in *living* each moment. The hand of death is present in reliance on routine, on passive innocuous repetition. Life is *not* repetition. To do anything well, we need technique, but not a technique deadened by habit – rather, a technique that is being constantly *refined*, employing *good* habits as a means of time-saving and as the very basis of continuity and improvement.

When I see the deft hands of my dentist, I know that hundreds of times they have gone through certain procedures, and experienced situations both difficult and easy. This gives me a sense of comfort and security. But a delicate balance needs to be maintained between the assurance of a well-trained hand

and mind, and a technique *alive* in the service of interpreting life, ready at all times to adjust, to rethink, to react anew.

The other day, when we were talking together, I used the image of a canoe being paddled through rapids – this is how I see my school. From time to time we have to deal with crises: a child is having real difficulty with his studies; or is behaving unpredictably; or has been upset by sad news from his parents, who may be thousands of miles away. Then we have to balance the needs of the one with the needs of the total community. Is it useful to have an element of the difficult in the school? To what extent is it strengthening? To what extent is it disrupting? And what about the child's musical talent? Will his value as a person and his potential as a musician prompt us to do our best to contain the difficulty?

A crisis such as this cannot be resolved by routine or by regulations. It can only be resolved by the living community, meeting together, feeling and thinking together, deciding together. We had an example of a problem of this kind a few weeks ago, and in the end we decided to keep the boy. A special concert had been arranged for children below a certain age, and this boy was among them. All the teachers were there and they felt that his playing warranted the effort of putting up with him and the difficulties he was presenting.

What is the yardstick by which you can measure a problem like this? Certainly not a cut-and-dried standard; I would call it an informed, mature, mutually-evolved commitment, on the part of the teachers and to a certain extent the older children. The decision they take imposes a responsibility and a challenge, and contains a hope and faith that the course they have chosen is the right one.

In every small group or community there exists a guiding ethos: not as formal as a law, not the judgement of a jury – because the people are actually assessing themselves – it is nonetheless a composite, coherent fabric, woven from the experience and ideals of the participants, and, in our case, the shared concept of the school, and the need to meet certain standards, academic and musical. Furthermore, our school is part of a wider society which has not yet abandoned humane features – and I hope never will – the result of many centuries of evolution.

At our school we have never met anyone, whether from local government, from party politics, or the Ministry of Education, who was a cipher or a policing-type or a cold, anonymous bureaucrat. On the contrary, we have met *real* people, with understanding and with interest in our work and aims.

147

This has brought forth from our side the desire to co-operate and show our sense of responsibility towards the country as a whole. Our reciprocal understanding with government can best be understood in terms of *anticipation.*

In a crude society there is no sensitive and understanding anticipation on either side. The result is that everyone takes what he can, as often as he can. There is a constant *rough* exchange of greeds, with inevitable suspicion and protectionism.

Our experience at the school is that we and the Government each anticipate the wishes of the other. Mutual anticipation is one of the most telling hallmarks of civilization – not waiting until a situation has hardened or until there is no room for movement, no margin for flexibility of decision. Everyone who is part of this civilized tradition is aware of the reaction that will be created by what he says and does. Unfortunately this may not so often happen in political or international circles, but in human relationships at our school it happens consistently.

We have no constitution, no creed that all who join us shall show only love. There is no formality, no belonging to a secret brotherhood. On the contrary, our school – I would like to think – is an expression of what is most open and valuable in England's heritage, a product of her ages-old growth and experience. I cannot imagine that the school would have developed as well in any other country.

So many of our actions and activities are done unconsciously. Sometimes people obey their better selves, and sometimes their worst selves; behaviour is guided to a large extent by instinct, habit, and conditioning. In an age of stress, when we are confronted by conflicting theories and factions, it is more than ever important to be *aware* of what we are trying to defend, and the standards we are trying to live up to.

We have gained support from so many quarters because people are yearning for reassurance: to see children working well; making good progress, together and individually; acting perfectly normally, courteously, and with an appropriate degree of independence; being well-informed about national and global issues; and able to enjoy sport in the traditional English way. Our school is now regarded as a continuation and embodiment of the

Opposite: With students from his school who, in 1976, played at the British Embassy in Washington at the Queen's request, to mark the U.S.A.'s bi-centennial year.

best English-boarding-school tradition.

Lord Donaldson [formerly Minister for the Arts] and other members of the then Government visited us recently, and there is interest in creating schools along similar lines for the teaching of sport. England is now caught up in an aggressively competitive world contrary to her whole way of thinking. But the English have been an adventurous people who were in equilibrium with a vast part of the world, through seafaring, exploration and colonies. A pattern of hundreds of years has now faded away, and England is turned in on herself. The pressures of international competition are being *forced* on the English.

There *is* a competitive element at the school: every child has a strong desire to improve, but not at the expense of others; and they are willing to *learn* from each other. From the very beginning, when three of our earliest students left and went to the Royal Academy, there has been a remarkable spirit of goodwill and affection, a real *camaraderie*, in the school. That year, all three departing students won major prizes. One of them said: 'I really don't deserve this. ——plays better than I do.'

We have a very flexible curriculum. Music of course comes first but it is essential that the children sit their 'O' and 'A' levels. They usually pass with remarkably high grades, even though they spend only about half the time than other children do on the same subjects. Our students are not going to become chemists and yet they are fascinated by chemistry. They assemble small computers. They build gliders. They know all about the birds, insects, and flowers, that are to be seen in our part of the country; they study in the same spirit as the English naturalists have done, not only as part of their own development, but simply because they find it a fascinating subject. They study French or German or Hebrew or astronomy in the same way, with the same sense of lively enquiry – not because it will help their future career, not in order to accumulate enough points so that they will be promoted to the next class. The result is that they tend to pass in these subjects more easily than other children do, who feel that their studies, their exams, are an obligation, a necessity, something that has to be done for self-survival.

Our children's music studies have the same range and the same joy as their other subjects do. They sing, compose, play chamber and orchestral music, and do solo work. We do not set out to produce a breed of students specially conceived and nurtured to win the Brussels Competition. We do not set out to produce students who, if they don't become virtuosi, regard themselves as failures – as tends to happen in Russia, and to a lesser extent in America.

Our students will go on to be – some are already – excellent orchestral and chamber-music players; some will become teachers. Already three of our former students are teaching part-time at the school.

We do our best to look after the total well-being of the children. The food is the most wholesome available, and some of it is grown on our own land. We use no white flour and no white sugar. Over the years we have had hardly any major sickness.

RD: I gathered that from the matron when I was talking with her the other day. She said that the children are much healthier than children of comparable age elsewhere.

YM: This is an indication that our diet and general routine are right. There are many things still to be improved. I am concerned with their posture, their manner of breathing, the way they walk. Life is a composite of all these elements. The books we read are as important as the food we eat. Our attitude of mind is as important as our digestion; indeed, one affects the other. A school – especially a boarding school – which doesn't take into account *everything* to do with the children's welfare is not fulfilling its obligations.

We fall short. There are still some flat-footed children at the school, and I insist that they be given the proper exercises and spend some time walking on their toes, so as to increase the arch of the foot. Everything is important – just as, in the interpretation of music, every note is important, has its own place and justification, and is related to all the other notes.

The children are very hardy. After playing the most delicate musical instruments, they go out of doors for rigorous sporting activity. A wide range of physical expression is vital because those who cosset themselves, seldom go outside, and burrow endlessly in subtleties of mind and art, lose the vigour which every musician requires.

One of the most important features of our day is the morning assembly. A week or so ago *The Times* published a letter of mine about it. From a meeting of assistant headmasters, one of them, a man of obvious integrity, had been reported as saying that daily religious services in schools were meaning less and less to children. He suggested that it would be far better to have a service only once a week, led by a truly convinced and devout person.

I then wrote, describing what we do at my school, where a number of religions are represented. I said I felt that the essential ingredients of a beginning-of-the-day assembly were singing – so good for the lungs and the communal spirit – and then a reading, by the headmaster or a guest, from any part of literature, eastern or western, philosophical, mystical, historical, religious. This is followed by a minute of silence.

Our morning assembly sets its seal on the day, with the whole community having shared an experience in which everyone was equal, and in which everyone has to some extent been moved, stimulated, integrated. The little children are there too and they sit quietly. We don't attempt to explain or expound on the reading, and some of the younger ones may not understand

'Teaching is a living relationship, of give and take, of mutual learning.'

much of it, but as they get older something of what they have heard will remain.

RD: Perhaps the school's day is itself an expansion of the reading.

YM: Exactly.

I must show you an article I read recently, which has given me a new idea for the school. It describes a community – I think it is somewhere in Malaysia – which has a long-established tradition of taking children's dreams seriously, and of allotting a particular time each day, probably early in the morning, for the sharing and elucidation of the previous night's dreams. A child is helped, for example, to understand and come to terms with some deep resentment he may have felt towards another member of the community. Those who were involved in the dream then enact a form of reconciliation.

This sounds to me like a very practical and organic way of resolving psychological problems which otherwise would remain buried, only to reappear later in an inappropriate or harmful way.

What we bury in our psyche sometimes reaches fertile ground. We need motive power of every description: disequilibrium sometimes produces remarkable and constructive results. But at the same time we need recourse to methods which can correct and relieve extreme feelings, extreme events.

RD: Working with dreams is such a delicate process. I feel sure that, in a communal setting, individual privacy should always be respected: every child should have the automatic right not to relate part of a dream which he felt was too personal to reveal.

YM: We know from the Oxford Group and from practices in Chinese society that public confessions can bring a certain amount of relief, especially, perhaps, to people who imagine they are singled out by fate and are the only ones to be troubled in a particular way. I should find public confession uncomfortable and embarrassing. But dreams come from a more remote level, beyond one's conscious awareness.

RD: Yes, and as Jung has pointed out – paradox though it may appear, in view of the seemingly bizarre form and content of some dreams – dreams are actually more objective, less liable to distortion, than the thoughts we have when we are awake.

YM: For that very reason, you are not exposing your conscious thoughts to public view; you are describing something you have *received*, an objective message, as you rightly say, which occurred in your mind when you were asleep. You alone are not responsible for what you dream: the whole community shares responsibility for the timing and content of your dreams, which result from your total subjective experience of life.

I find this whole subject most illuminating and full of possibilities. I intend to discuss it with the headmaster of our school, Peter Renshaw.

RD: From what I have seen of your school, one element is less present than in many other schools. There is much less fear: less fear of punishment, less fear of an impersonal system, less fear of being unrewarding to teach. If, as at an orthodox music academy, a child sees his teacher for only half an hour, three times a week, he is for many reasons likely to enter the teacher's room somewhat apprehensively. But at your school the children see their teachers on many different occasions every day, and so music lessons do not have inordinate focus and expectation; they are part of the whole day, the whole way of life.

YM: Yes, the boarding school is a great institution. At day schools, the music teachers come for a few hours, see a few pupils, and then go away again, without being able to develop any personal feeling for the building, the setting, the rooms themselves. A boarding school has the advantage of providing a total atmosphere in which the whole of life proceeds – working, talking, eating, sleeping, rehearsing, rejoicing – and where music, the expression of wholeness of life, is studied and played.

I have no wish to disparage the great schools of music, but I feel they are more suitable for older students. And for a young child in his formative years, who is at an ordinary day school, the learning of music cannot be related to the whole of life as it can at a boarding school, where study is merged into the life of a community, where difficulties and pleasures are shared, and where the children have the constant stimulus of others equally talented.

The only fear they know is of not living up to what they expect of themselves. This can be a healthy form of fear, although it sometimes drives them to work harder than we want them to. We have had to discourage several children from working for a couple of hours before breakfast!

Unless it is something private that needs to be confined to a meeting between headmaster and child, problems are usually aired among all the children. Then the fear is of letting other people down, and perhaps the school as well. The children have no formal allegiance, there is no school flag to salute, but when they play in the school orchestra they all want the performance to be as good as possible. They don't say to themselves: 'Now we have to hold aloft the standards of the school.' Their dedication, the quality of their playing, just *is*.

Life is so much better when things just *are*, than when they are *supposed* to be. Ideally, we should be guided, impelled, not by deliberate thought or ambition but by an *innate* need for expression: you work hard because you *want* to work hard.

I have little faith in resolutions: they are often adopted when a person is under pressure; they cannot fit every human situation; and they can cause terrible guilt if infringed. I am always wary of *final* statements. I have to *live* the difficulty, *live* the relationship.

RD: What do you look and listen for when selecting from among the many children who want to come to your school?

YM: The staff are gathered together and we consider the child's whole approach. Is he musical? Can he sing and carry a tune? Does he have a sense of rhythm? Does he have a good sense of pitch? Can he sight-read? Does he really *love* music? In his playing, does he convey even a small amount of spontaneity and real expression?

Then we look at the child's co-ordination, which is vital in any physical pursuit. We look at the child's general appearance; and his liveliness of response when we talk to him. Some of the children may feel nervous and embarrassed by any questions put to them, but if they have already expressed themselves adequately through music we can discount a certain degree of shyness.

What we look for is a balance of all these factors; no child does all of them well. Some children are irresistible – in personality, in eagerness, in their desire to work and to learn.

If a child comes from a family that loves music, and if one or both parents have had some experience of playing an instrument, the chances of success are greater. But we have had a few children from comparatively unmusical families.

RD: Do you ever speculate about how this happens?

With Robert Masters, violinist, concertmaster and a teacher at the school.

YM: Children today hear a great deal of music, of all kinds. They meet and are influenced by other children, at school and in their neighbourhood. They have more and earlier opportunities, than previous generations had, to break away from the parental mould. This greater independence enables children to develop interests which may be quite different from those of their parents. But on the whole the children at our school come from a musical background.

RD: Presumably the next stage is to assess the source of the child's motivation: how much is coming from within and how much is coming from the ambitions of parents?

YM: Yes, children who have been pushed too hard by their parents find enormous relief at the school: some would prefer to stay with us throughout the year, and not go back home during the holidays. But the majority of our children are relatively happy at home and want to go and see their parents and family.

The school has its own kind of tension. The children accomplish a great deal of work. They are not leading lives of carefree indulgence. Quite the contrary. They achieve more, they carry much more burden of activity of many different kinds – if you can call it a burden – than children of their age in most other schools.

RD: I should be grateful if you would tell me more about the parents, and the problems that arise when they invest too much – emotionally – in their gifted children.

YM: The parents are often in a dilemma: they want the best for the child; and they may see it as a major sacrifice on their part to allow him to go to a boarding school. Sometimes the child's leaving home is not a problem; it may even be a relief for the parents and the child.

Every parent wants his child to be successful, and only a parent who can take an enlightened and objective view draws the distinction between his ambition for the child, and the child's own desire for self-expression and fulfilment. On the whole, the parents of our students do not have unreasonably high expectations of their children: I find this less of a problem here in England than it might be in America or Russia.

Even the parents of our Asian children, who in a way are sacrificing more than others because of the distance, and whose hopes are fed by that sacrifice – even they are not continually writing to us, wanting to have progress reports. I think all the parents realize that their children are well looked after, and that the school is a good place for them to be.

RD: Over the past years, which nationalities have been represented at the school?

YM: We have a very talented Formosan boy, whom you heard at our end-of-term concert. In addition to children from all over Britain, we have had a couple of pianists from Singapore, and we now have a Swiss boy. We have had Indians, Israelis, French, Japanese, Italians, Americans and Germans.

RD: How do you deal with sadness of failure in the selection process – both the child's and the parents' sadness?

YM: The parents realize that we have only a limited number of places each year: that is part of the risk of applying. If there is a child we particularly regret having to turn down, or a family who warrant special commiseration and compassion, we give what advice we can, such as the name of another school to try for.

RD: No doubt you have a sixth sense for detecting that aspect of temperament which will help a child, and later the adult, to survive the struggles of the artistic life.

YM: More important than anything else is the love of music. If the child has in his mind an image of the sound he would like to hear himself play, and if that image is strong enough, then he will rise to it.

RD: One of the few remaining taboos is the subject of discipline. And yet it seems to me that to have a central discipline in your life – be it music or some other activity which is fulfilling and self-enlarging – gives freedom and openness to all facets of your existence.

YM: Discipline is essential to the harmony and success of any undertaking. Ideally, we should aim for *self*-discipline; but at first, at a young age, we need to learn discipline by example, from a person of distinctive character.

I fear that 'discipline', like many other words such as 'peace' and 'courage', tends these days to be given a fixed meaning, as if it were an element you could transplant. We tend to think of discipline in the military sense in which every individual is a replica, each a model of self-control, precision and order.

Discipline is the ability to repeat a given action deliberately and correctly. Discipline is thus the most economical way of achieving a given purpose. Discipline offers the shortest and simplest way, the way with the least detours, the least eccentricities – once the complexities have been attended to, analysed, reduced.

Routine is a form of repetitive action lacking a sense of new purpose; but discipline is something more. The distinctive quality of discipline is of effort related to a clear and chosen purpose, resulting in greater ease, reliability, and security of achievement.

Certain people, as soon as they aim at something with all their heart, automatically seek the easiest, most economical way of achieving their goal. But some temperaments are not given to discipline; by compensation, they may be more spontaneous, more imaginative, perhaps having a rich fantasy life. It may take them longer to complete a particular activity; but the more creative that activity is, the richer their achievement may be.

A balance needs to be kept between discipline and creativity: they can be mutually helpful. Balance is required in any human effort, enabling you to gain the best from both sides. Whereas as soon as you are out of balance, you are in an extreme position, and you give yourself or your group to one side exclusively. This means that you rely on the opposition to balance you: your *raison d'être* is dependent on your antagonist. The penalty of going over to one side exclusively, and of existing only through and by your enemy, is that you are then committed to fight. Those who are strong-willed are these days more usually associated with a one-sided view. This is where the twin evils of prejudice and intolerance are born.

The strongest character is the person who can step the farthest possible out of balance and yet retrieve himself. If you stay in the very middle of the scales, you will feel virtually no movement at all, and the chances are that you will lead a rather dull life. Creativity requires an intuitive free abandon, albeit within the discipline of certain forms and structures. The larger the area in which you can abandon yourself, while retaining a degree of balance, the more creative you are.

RD: Do you have any particular people in mind?

YM: Beethoven and Bartók. Bartók had an amazing blend of discipline and imagination. Upstairs I have six volumes containing the results of Bartók's research, grouping, analysis, and cataloguing, of the folk music of Romania, Hungary, North Africa, the whole Balkan peninsula. All his work was done with painstaking methodology. First of all, he went into the countryside, got to know the villagers, and elicited from the oldest of them all the folk songs they could remember. Next he discovered variations, within a village and between villages. Then he tabulated all these songs, categorizing them according to their rhythms, moods, melodies, and the particular festivals or season when they were sung.

This incredibly detailed and scholarly work was done by a man who composed the most dramatic – even savage – music imaginable. No matter

how savage his music, he never renounced the basic elements of rhythm, logic, and structure. Here we can see an example of discipline and natural, instinctive forces in balance.

Clutching his first-generation phonograph, travelling by foot or on a cart or a donkey, visiting remote villages, steeping himself in folklore, loving the earth and its produce, loving animals, loving everything related to the organic, Bartók was a latter-day European version of the Red Indian. He analysed every track, every footstep: he worked out how long it had been there and who might have left it and where it was leading.

Towards the end of his life, Bartók was invited by the University of Washington, in Seattle, to make a study of the Red Indian tribes of the northwest. He would have revelled in this work, even at his age [early sixties], if he had been in good health.

Bartók devoted an immense span of time to his work on the folk music of the Balkans, from his early fieldwork to his final task in a room at Columbia University, organizing and collating all his material. At the same time as this methodical work, Bartók was composing works such as the Solo Sonata for me, and the *Concerto for Orchestra*, thus displaying an astonishing range of temperament, imagination and patience. One of the surest measures of true stature is the capacity to *encompass* a long stretch of time – between one's dream, one's vision, and its realization.

RD: From his diaries, we know that Beethoven also drew much inspiration from walks in the countryside.

YM: Every creative person goes to the *source* of creation. Unfortunately for us today, many of our sources are second-hand. But Bartók, like other great composers before him, delighted in natural phenomena and in the art of the people. To be at one with your background – climatic, linguistic and cultural – is of prime importance to a creative person. The countryside was *everything* to Schubert and to Beethoven.

The inventive talents of Thomas Edison were entirely at one with that period in American expansion when everything was considered possible, a time of almost child-like curiosity and hope. Nature is still full of mystery: we see, but we don't see; and though we hear, we don't hear. To be creative, we

Opposite: Bartók: 'an amazing blend of discipline and imagination.'

need to regain a child's way of seeing – with eyes that are not *blasé*, not blinkered by habit, not blinded by concepts, notions, interpretations.

Just think for a moment of the number of different ways of perceiving a tree: the many possible uses of its wood; the birds and insects it houses; the transformation of rain and sunlight into energy and growth; the changes in colour; its seasonal clothing and disrobing; the cellular constituents, the sap, the bark, the rings, testament of the tree's age.

Then we have the poetic and mystical aspects of a tree, and its ages-old symbolism: representing growth, strength, protection, family, rootedness. Each one of these aspects contains truths; and each one of these truths is veiled by ignorance and habitual ways of observing. There is no *one* truth about a tree. A tree is an *endless* source of wonder.

Schubert and Beethoven *belonged* to the countryside around Vienna; to those beautiful forests where the gentleness of one season swiftly alternates with the rigours of the next; they belonged to that geographical point where east meets west, where the Turks came and were twice repulsed; where south meets north, Italy meets Germany; where the Romans gave way to the Magyars; where the pampas of Europe, the rich flat lands of Hungary, the *pushta*, meet the edge of the Alps. These cross-fertilizations *were* the wealth of the Vienna of those days: her power and influence were more cultural than military.

In the music of Schubert and Beethoven we are made aware, in depth, of human pain and human tragedy. Radical social change and the great upheaval in Europe are indirectly reflected in Beethoven's music, but his artistic integrity remained unblemished. He depicts the individual as remaining supreme – to observe, to struggle, and, in the end, to triumph.

9

REFLECTIONS

RD: The other day I was thinking about the variety of national and cultural influences in your life: your parents Jewish–Russian; your birthplace and early years in America; your European travels and teachers. Was there any particular time when you felt either that these influences needed to be integrated in some way, or that they *were* being integrated by a natural process of living and experiencing? Perhaps music has helped to harmonize these cultural lines.

YM: Yes, you are right. Music – using, as it does, the whole body, the nerves and muscles, the intellect, imagination, and spirit – is a very good integrator.

The two most important influences – apart from music itself, which works and heals subliminally – were on the one hand the philosophy of Constantin Brunner and on the other, Diana: Brunner helped me in the realm of theory; Diana, in the practical experience of daily life.

I was immediately attracted by Brunner's *global* conception: the way he links matter and spirit; the way he sees 'to feel, to want, and to know' as parts of one basic impulse; his vision of plants, trees, animals, people, the arts, as aspects of one unity, all related, all mutually influential.

Brunner revolutionized my thinking. He enabled me to see that opposites – good and bad, body and soul, work and play, night and day – are only *apparent* opposites; and that events and experiences which on the surface seem disjointed, even inimical, do have meaningful connections.

Diana's influence is in the living of each day. Before I met her, my life had been self-propelled by music. I had missed a great deal of the kind of experience which establishes realities: the ability to assess other people; the ability to steer a sensible and steady course through a hazardous passage of one's life; the ability to translate a feeling of compassion into a realistic way of helping.

The art of helping – and at the same time allowing the other person to retain his sense of independence – is a profoundly difficult art, needing

infinite flexibility. Sometimes you have to cause temporary hurt in order to help; sometimes you can help in an indirect way; sometimes help is easily given and easily received, if all that is wanted is a little nudge – a music lesson, a small loan, a letter of introduction, an hour to discuss a problem. Deeper, longer-term needs are much more complex: the complexity inheres not only in the need itself but in the ever-fluctuating relationship between the helper and the person being helped. On the whole I tend to find children easier to help than adults.

RD: I wonder if perhaps a third integrating factor in your life was your setting up home here in Highgate in the late Fifties, making London the base for your many activities?

YM: Yes. In Highgate Village, Diana and I feel more part of a community than we did in California. I value being able to conduct all my activities within a given area, among people who really *belong* to one another.

Day by day, my whole life is centred in this great city: recordings, my school, charity projects, *Live Music Now* – all are based here. So are my children, my agent and his staff, the Arts Council, my orchestral colleagues and good friends from many other professions – scientists, doctors, artists, politicians.

I am both fascinated and repelled by New York. I adore Paris. Many other cities I love, but I love London most of all. My *life* is here. Other cities, other countries – however well I know them, however many friends I may have there, and however long I may stay – they are only places to *visit*. London contains the full spectrum, the whole tapestry of my life.

RD: Are there any types of people, or types of behaviour, that annoy you?

YM: Any artificiality, pomposity; anyone who over-rates himself because he has an official position – nothing irritates me more than the behaviour of the little *Gauleiter*.

Another thing that irritates me is lack of vision. A great legal mind is to be admired; what I dislike is a narrow legalistic approach, which judges a human being or a situation on the basis of a single criterion, often a prejudiced one; a mind fossilized by habit, which rejects any challenge or opposing view, which lacks the courage to defend basic principles of freedom and justice; a mind not guided by curiosity, respect, humility.

I most admire a really enlightened diagnostician, someone like our family friend, Dr Carl Goldman. When he examines a patient, he takes into account dozens of factors – such as skin tone, manner of breathing, and mental state – quite apart from the usual analysis of blood and urine. His searching mind and senses, his wide experience, his ability to evaluate a number of different symptoms – these insights enable him to construct a working hypothesis, which can later be enlarged or modified.

I admire people who are not deluded by the vanity of their own ideas; people who are willing to discard an idea and, if necessary, change course; people who have the gift of *seeing more*.

RD: You were talking the other day about the high code of honour among the aristocracy at a certain period of European history. What ideals do you hold dearest in the conduct of your own life?

YM: Trust and honesty between human beings, and a willingness to learn to understand the rôle of time. Our aims in life need to be pursued constantly, but results are neither instant nor inevitable. Therefore an element of faith is needed in continuing any work, any career, any natural, intuitive inclination which is neither altogether selfish, nor altogether altruistic. In addition I aspire to a certain aesthetic sense of balance which merges into personal morality. These are the guiding lines of my life – but I am the first to admit that I will never match up to them.

No success or victory is absolute: some turn out to be hollow; for them all, there is sooner or later a price to be paid. It is always preferable to pay in *advance*; yet it is often possible, if sometimes difficult, to pay up later. All successes are the result of many factors combining together, including chance and coincidence. So I *cannot* take credit for any achievements, such as they may be. They are the result of many fortuitous circumstances: background, parents, luck, unsought experience; the rare good fortune of meeting Diana and Enesco; the thousands of things that happen by instinct and fate, by a walk, by a chance meeting, by reading a poem that sparks off a new idea.

I have not always drawn full benefit from good fortune, nor always come to the right conclusions, nor learned the particular lesson that life at various times was seeking to teach me.

Nor have I gone through life without hurting many people. I have never caused pain deliberately or out of vindictiveness, but nonetheless just as effectively as if it had been deliberate. I frequently ponder over this whole subject. As much suffering is due to misguided goodwill as to intentional harm. And much suffering is due to misapplied or narrow or irrelevant principle. The kindest people often cause the greatest tragedies.

I know my limitations of instinct and of character. The limitations of my knowledge are self-evident: I never attended a school; I never had a rigorous, disciplined training of a scholarly kind. My handwriting reveals a certain impatience; it is not the script of a scholar. If my mind is on something else, begrudging the time I am having to spend writing, or if I am afraid to lose the thread of an idea, my handwriting becomes almost illegible.

I am not a really well-read person. In music, I have not played all the quartets of Beethoven or Bartók, Mozart or Haydn. During my years in New York, at a very formative stage of my life, I went to as many Toscanini

Menuhin with Kodály and Gary Bertini.

concerts as I could, and heard many times all the Beethoven and Brahms symphonies, but I still haven't heard all the symphonies of Bruckner and Mahler. I certainly don't know a vast number of the cantatas of Bach; and the fact that I don't play the piano, which is a great handicap, has prevented me from playing the 48 *Preludes and Fugues* and thus assimilating them through my fingers as well as through my mind.

When I study a work, I search for the structure, the sequence of the composer's thought. This deliberate process may yield some benefits which are denied to a musician who can study and learn a score at the piano; but this may just be an apology for a gift I don't possess. And I don't have anything like the memory for music of an Enesco or a Mitropoulos.

So much for the limitations of my knowledge. What about character? I have made many mistakes. I am not one of those strong-willed people who chase after a desire, regardless of cost to himself and others. There are very few things – either to achieve or to defend – that I would give up everything for, even my life.

Being able to see both sides can be very weakening. It is possible to have *too* much understanding; but I constantly try to find a balance. I think I can defend a personal conviction without losing sight of the value to be found on both sides. For instance, I was invited by the Debating Society at Cambridge to take part in an evening when the motion was 'Art is élitist'. The supporters of *both* sides wanted me!

The pyramids are unquestionably élitist, but the cathedral in Chartres is less so; and folk music belongs entirely to the people. Some of the greatest works of art could never have been attempted without an aristocracy that had the capital to encourage creativity and the leisure to enjoy its results. Therefore I felt I couldn't defend one argument or the other exclusively, but would take part provided we sought a consensus of all the valid points of view inherent in the question. For the participants to remain each on his own side at the end of the discussion, as if nothing had happened, seemed to me a waste of time. I wanted us to construct – from our diversity – a coherent understanding and attitude.

Sometimes I am tempted to delay making a decision, until I know more about the issue or until I feel more convinced one way or the other. Sometimes I don't trust my intuition enough: I am thinking particularly of the years of uncertainty towards the end of my first marriage. If I had taken the initiative when I could and should have done, I would have been able to marry Diana earlier.

My failings are part of my whole character. I know I cannot have one part without the other, but life is a continuous effort of self-refinement: to strengthen the better parts and shed the weak.

So, in answer to your question about the salient principles or guide lines of my life, I cannot respond as someone who feels he has been highly successful or believes that almost everything in his life has turned out satisfactorily. It would be misleading for me to get up on a pedestal and talk about my life from there, but I do believe – as one among other fallible mortals – in the importance of mutual trust and in being as honest as possible with oneself and with one's neighbour. The complications of untrustworthiness are terrible.

Trust is to life and love what discipline and economy are to the fine arts. Even though periods of architecture in India, and our own Baroque era, spawned opulent and extravagant ornamentation, with carvings on every inch of available space, nonetheless we can assume that the technique of the carver was economical.

Imagination must be allowed to be freewheeling, unencumbered, un-tethered. For the next stage of the creative process – to translate the vision effectively – you need the economy of discipline. In the same way, love is *in essence* free, boundless, and all-embracing; but love needs the discipline of trustworthiness as a means of making society possible, and enabling people to live and work together.

Even the bargaining that takes place in an eastern *souk* – where you are not expected to pay the initial asking price – is not a form of untrustworthiness; it is a game in the art of compromise in which both sides know the rules. The seller starts by asking perhaps twice as much as he expects to receive. Eventually the two sides meet somewhere in the middle.

Bargaining – that is to say, edging closer and closer to the real value as perceived by both seller and buyer – is a kind of parable typifying man's eternal search, in the open field of life, for the average, for the middle way, for an agreed truth. In fact bargaining is fairer than a fixed-price system. Fixed prices don't take into account the individual buyer's capacity to pay, nor the individual retailer's profit margin. A fixed price is essential in an industrialized society, in which goods are produced *en masse*; but where hand-made objects are sold, often by the carpet-maker or weaver himself, the institution of bargaining is perfectly natural and acceptable. Ultimately, personal intentions are every bit as important as prices.

RD: Do other people see you as you see yourself?

YM: That is a difficult question to answer. For one thing, I am not altogether sure how I see myself – that must make it even more difficult for others!

The public can form an opinion of me – as musician, husband, father – only on the basis of momentary impressions. For them to believe what they believe – and many see me as a relatively kind person, concerned for the well-being of others – they require very little fact. They believe because they *need* to believe. I provide a not-too-controversial personality on to whom they can fasten their belief. I am not misled or taken in by this. It places a responsibility on me but would not be a decisive factor in a choice between my own principles and fulfilling other people's expectations of me.

A story about Casals will illustrate this. I saw him after the war in Prades, France. He had spent the years of conflict in a simple way, gathering his own firewood, and being visited every so often by Catalans from across the border who looked on him as their leader. After the war he was regarded as *the* symbol of anti-Fascism, which indeed he deserved to be. But among the people who put him on this pedestal were a group of American musicians for whom the art of music and the art of self-advertising were inextricably joined together.

Casals told me about his war years and admitted that he admired some Germans – Furtwängler, notably – but had little respect for a few well-known French musicians who had lived in comparative luxury during the Vichy régime. Casals felt that, by contrast, he had suffered for holding on to his convictions, refusing to bow down to the Nazis. He was once arrested by an SS squad but thankfully was soon released without having been taken from his home.

Casals respected Furtwängler not only as a man of integrity but as a fine musician. So I asked Casals if he would like to record the Brahms Double Concerto with me, with Furtwängler as conductor. 'Yes, certainly', he said, but the correspondence dragged on for two or three years. Whenever I tried to finalize a date, there was always an obstacle. Finally I received a letter in which he said: 'You will recall that I told you nothing would give me more pleasure than to record with Furtwängler. I still feel he is a man of integrity. However, I am seen by my colleagues in New York as a symbol of anti-Fascism, and I would let them down if I played under Furtwängler. They wouldn't understand.'

Casals was trapped by his followers, a danger that faces everyone in public life. Nothing can be more embarrassing to a priest or a rabbi than to be revered by his congregation – to whom he preaches noble words – and to be

Menuhin with Pablo Casals.

seen in another and more realistic way by his family and closest friends.

From the early years onwards, my parents drummed into me: 'You are your own best critic as well as your own severest critic! And so when nice elderly ladies used to come into the artist's room after a concert in San Francisco, when I was a boy, and hug me, saying, 'Dear Yehudi, you were wonderful. You are the true successor of Paganini,' I thanked them graciously but didn't let their praise give me an inflated view of my own worth.

For some years – around the period of my first marriage – I was numb, and for a variety of reasons. I concentrated very largely on music, tours, wartime concerts. With hindsight, I can see that the tours were too long, and I didn't have a big enough repertoire to maintain a fresh approach in my playing. In this, my son Jeremy has a much better balance: his ratio of study time compared to the number of his concert performances is much healthier than mine ever was.

Even then, I still had many wonderful opportunities for stimulus and renewal. I often heard Heifetz, Elman and Kreisler. I had that memorable season of opera in Salzburg with my father. I came to love Schubert through listening to the *Lieder*. I played a great deal of chamber music, especially during two periods: in Ville d'Avray, Paris, with Enesco, every Thursday; and in 'Alma', our California home, during the first years of the war. Lastly, and very importantly, Toscanini's concerts continue to live within me.

As a conductor I still have much to learn. I have now started to conduct opera, something I longed to do for many years. Opera gives the best possible training to a conductor: you have to keep in contact with the stage, the orchestra, the voice line, and the words. What I found particularly difficult, the very first time I conducted accompanied recitative, was the bringing in of those sharp chords of comment from the orchestra: they have to be rhythmically precise, and at the same time compatible with the individual expression of the singer. I had already begun to find this less of a problem in the second and third performances of the opera – *Così fan tutte* – and no doubt I will continue to learn more.

I hope that my image of myself is unclouded by either praise or criticism. I have had my share of severe criticism, some of it well-justified, though in my experience critics seldom ascribe correct reasons for an artist's below-par performance.

Thankfully, I have been the subject of very little prejudice or ill-will, but there *has* been some, possibly because of my Jewish origins, possibly due to envy of a richly favoured career and life – at least as seen by an outsider.

I don't waste my time dwelling on this, wondering why people see me the way they do. I feel it is humiliating and degrading to trade in arguments and evaluations of other people's motives. The important thing is to be oneself, and to play and communicate as best one can. In the final analysis, I take responsibility for myself.

Naturally, I prefer to read comment which is favourable. I cannot pretend I wasn't pleased when Diana showed me Martin Cooper's review of my recent recording of Bach's solo sonatas. I was *very* pleased. I felt he understood what I was trying to convey through the music. And I would have been very unhappy if the recording had found no favour with anybody.

RD: It has always seemed to me that there are two outstanding privileges of a career in the arts: first, that your art offers a constant source of self-renewal; second, that you have a profession to which you can devote the whole of your lifespan. Unlike a businessman who retires in middle age, you have a whole lifetime to find new avenues for your gift.

YM: Yes, exactly. And this is why a hobby is so important. Everyone should be an amateur, in love with his special subject, and this attitude should be encouraged from the earliest years. Crafts, and even architecture, should be taught in every school. I know of an architect, Michael Tollitt, who takes young children out into the country at weekends, and with whatever material is at hand – branches, small bits of wood, bricks, clay – they build huts and even miniature houses.

I think everybody should learn to create something, no matter what the quality. I fear that the fine arts have been raised on to a pedestal, with the result that until recently crafts have been neglected. The two must be brought closer together again, because one is an outgrowth of the other.

Music should be made available to everybody, players as well as listeners, and this is why I am promoting a new project, *Live Music Now*, with the support of the Arts Council. The aim is to bring music into the lives of people of all ages who – by reason of cost or distance or inability to leave an institution, such as a hospital, prison, or retirement home – would not normally be able to attend a concert.

Young musicians will be encouraged to visit schools, explain the use of their instruments, talk informally about music, and play for the children. This is one of the ways in which music can become more part of daily life. At the same time, crafts must be reactivated, resuscitated. There is enormous scope for co-operatives, for people to work at home, and take pride in their work.

RD: All your life you have given freely of your time to charities and voluntary agencies. How do you select from among the many good causes that ask for your help?

YM: First, I have to believe in what they are doing; second, it is a matter of first come, first served – and of being able to fit the charity events into my schedule. I may answer: 'I am very sympathetic to your aims and work, but for the next two years my schedule is already overfilled.' Two years go by and I receive another letter, 'You kindly promised to consider playing for us in 19—,' by which time the *next* two years are now filled!

There is a constant flow of requests, and so many good works which I would love to help. This morning I received a letter from a very fine organization which helps families in Northern Ireland, asking if I would play on 11 July of this year at a benefit concert. I won't be in Britain on 11 July so the answer is simple, but I hope to be able to help them on some other occasion.

Sometimes two charity events coincide, each with its own importance. This happened a few months ago: the Save the Children Fund was celebrating the hundredth anniversary of the birth of its founder, Eglantyne Jebb, a remarkable woman; at the same time I received an invitation from the President of the World Jewish Congress, Dr Nahum Goldmann, to play at their convention in Geneva. Diana and I thought this would be a most interesting event for us to attend; it would enable us to feel the pulse of world Jewry.

I didn't think it would be possible to go to both events: one in London in the afternoon; the other in Geneva that same evening. However the Congress, very keen for Diana and I to come, made arrangements for us to be rushed to a small plane, immediately after the Save the Children Fund celebrations. I hadn't travelled in such luxury since the war, when I occasionally flew by private plane at the behest of an American general or admiral.

I chose to play one of Ernest Bloch's Solo Suites. This seemed the obvious choice for a number of reasons: they were his last works and had been dedicated to me; he was born in Geneva, host city for the Congress; having become a naturalized American, he was a fellow-countryman of mine; he was a Jew and a great deal of his music has Jewish associations.

Because of my sabbatical I was able to attend both the events. If I had been on tour – and they are planned at least two years in advance – this would have been impossible. My sabbatical has offered me the opportunity of doing some of the things kept at bay by a schedule which forbade intrusions. It has been intriguing for me to see how many personal interests, and how many requests, had been pigeonholed for so long. Perhaps I have yet to find the right balance.

The quandaries of life are sometimes more difficult than truly inescapable problems. Indeed, we tend to seek refuge in the inescapable as a way of opting for clear-cut decisions. Very often what we *consider* obligatory is in fact only an escape from what we really should be doing, but are avoiding through doubt, fear, indecision.

A musician's life can be an escape: into the security of music; into the pleasure and gratitude of thousands of people, a few of whom he will meet fleetingly after a concert. But the support of multitudes is no substitute for self-integration and the affection of close friends and family.

Life involves constant exchange. Every artistic person – whether creator or performer – is only *ostensibly* on the giving end of the exchange. In fact the giver is also the taker. Absolute giving does not exist. The earth doesn't give endlessly. What meets the eye is the giving. We see the soil yielding wheat and forests and flowers and grass, and we think of it as giving all the time. We tend to forget that the earth has to *receive*; has to refresh and renew itself; has to lie fallow for a time; has to be ploughed, watered, enriched, fed with new seed.

The eye misleads. We see a soloist standing in front of an audience, giving. But at the same time he is fulfilling *himself*. He is drawing energy and inspiration from the music. He is being given support by the audience and by his fellow-musicians, the orchestral players and the conductor. And, not least, this is his means of earning a living. A soloist is just a middleman between composer and audience. He is not even an improviser, as Indian musicians are. I give concerts because I love and feel music, and am convinced of its eternal value.

In addition to invitations to play at charity concerts, I receive many requests for written messages in support of various ventures. For example, I delight in being President of the Puffin Club, which encourages young people to write poetry, as well as many other pursuits, all challenging and wholesome. For a recent competition I chose a melody from *Don Giovanni*,

and Diana wrote a charming limerick. The children were asked to set the limerick to music and, conversely, to write words for the melody.

The inventiveness of children, their imagination, their poetry and painting, their pottery, their use of wood and other materials – the talent of children is formidable. Adults, all over the world, have under-rated the ability of children, and have often forced them into narrow educational channels.

One of my greatest satisfactions is to see the young children at my school expressing themselves, in music, in painting, in sports, even in farming. And I hope that my *Live Music Now* scheme will provide hundreds of new opportunities for young musicians to play all over the country.

RD: You have been speaking about how you choose which charities to support. I wonder if you would now like to reflect on the subject of choice in its widest sense.

YM: Choice is one of life's greatest challenges. I had to go through some terrible years when my first marriage was virtually finished: my Talmudic Jewish mind was wedged between the rigours of the Law and the dictates of the heart. There seemed to be no escape from my dilemma. For about three years I couldn't find the determination to decide what I wanted to do.

Choice is profoundly difficult, and that is why so many people think they would like a dictatorship – in the hope that this would relieve them of the problems of choice. Another self-deceptive way of gaining conviction is to unite against a scapegoat: you then enter a fool's paradise in which, justified by dogma, you indulge in prejudice, hate, and even violence, without a glimmer of doubt as to the rightness of your activity.

England now urgently needs to choose: she needs to select and balance the best of the old and the best of the new. We live in a precarious age; more and more people cling to the bureaucratic safety of routine work, with income linked to the cost-of-living index. This great island people who have sailed the seven seas with initiative and daring; who have loved and *sought* adventure; who have an emancipated way of thinking; who have a strong sense of team-work and *camaraderie* – all of this is evaporating, and either finding refuge in the bureaucrat's office or aggressive outlet with a terrorist gang. These are the two extremes of our day: both are unable to fulfil the needs of the individual and of society, one being too secure, and the other too disordered.

Some of the most able people, as in Northern Ireland, who tried to build bridges between the two sides, have been wantonly murdered. The world is on a knife edge, balanced between the forces of destruction and the forces of regeneration, between saving humanity or allowing mankind to destroy itself. What will be the decisive factor? What will tip the balance? Probably a mistake, a miscalculation, a catastrophe caused by nature, or some form of chance element.

RD: From an existentialist point of view, choice and chance are closely connected.

YM: We are conditioned by our past experiences. Choice, risk and sense of adventure, are made easier if we have the memory and assurance of even moderate success in the past. Choice is more difficult – for some, almost impossible – if we have been repeatedly disappointed.

At times we are all willing to surrender to what the fates have in store for us, as a counterblast to that side of us which longs for continuity, for the *known*. If you invited a crowd of 100,000 people to take part in a lottery, three large prizes might be sufficient inducement for most to join in. And even though 99,997 will feel frustrated at losing, few would be discouraged from trying a second time.

In the past, if you lost a large amount by gambling, you took your plight very seriously: you repaid the debt or you shot yourself. And I don't think many people of today gamble with a precious possession, as Paganini did with his Guarnerius.

Choice and chance are always at work, usually in a subtle and cumulative way. A seemingly modest choice or minor chance-event is compounded by time into new paths, each with its own commitments, its own vested interests, its own destiny – all of which will have started at a single place and moment in the remote past. Human history moves forward to *diverging* lines and backward to *converging* lines; the few becoming the many, and the many becoming the few.

Every moment in life is a new point of departure, an ending and a beginning, a convergence as well as a divergence. All that we are today is the result of tens of thousands of past actions, an interweaving of choices and chances, some grasped, many squandered.

RD: What is your attitude to money?

YM: I am in two minds about money. I wish it could be dispensed with! Money is a practical and fluid means of exchange for most transactions, but I do think there is a place for barter, even in an advanced society. Barter creates an opportunity for people to meet, and to exchange goods of real value, articles they themselves have made. Also barter preserves the relationship between urban man and the man who tills the soil.

Money gives some people a false sense of power, the lamentable, self-deluding idea of being able to command anything at any time. No matter how rich you may be, you cannot command art, you cannot command love.

I treat money as a useful means to get things done. I have been fortunate in being able to earn ever since I was a child, but I have never accumulated any capital. I have a ridiculously small amount of capital after half a century of work. I cannot afford to stop working for more than a year.

I realize the value of money, and I appreciate being able to live in Highgate, and have a car and the services of a wonderful secretary. Someone might say: 'This ought to give you more leisure time.' It doesn't. As soon as you have facilities, you use them. I hope that something of what I do is useful to society: the school, my *Live Music Now* scheme, and the many other projects that come my way. These days there are fewer and fewer people who can use their money in this way, and replace it.

I don't waste money on myself. I like to get useful things done, and I like to see people well rewarded for their work. I have to earn a great deal to do the things I want to do, for family, friends, and charitable purposes. I am by now fairly well versed in the fee structure for concerts and the rôle of managers and agents. I have known them for decades, so we seldom need to discuss business arrangements. I know what they are doing on my behalf, and can leave them to keep track of my concert bookings and financial position.

If you were to ask me the size of my bank balance, I would have to go and find out. If I give a normal year's concerts, I know I can afford certain things. But I don't think in money terms; I think only of music and of the various projects I am involved in. I am very fortunate in that way: I think in the manner of a third-generation millionaire, who takes it for granted that he can do what he wants to do, but in fact I am not even a *first*-generation millionaire!

RD: When talking about your school, you mentioned the morning assembly and its imprint on the rest of the day. How do you see the natural pattern of a day's activities?

YM: The need for survival breeds all kinds of defence, pretence, acquisitiveness, self-justification, competitiveness, and so forth. But we are born with certain harmonies and need to return to them. I always like to return to *instinctive* patterns; having discovered what they are, I can then try to adapt to them.

To be at one with the day's cycle can be of immense help in everything we do; then, regardless of what happens to us, we are still in tune with the reliability of the cycle. The beginning of each day is a reassuring phenomenon, especially if you live, as I did in childhood, close to the elements. In San Francisco I observed the dew on the early-morning grass, the arrival of sunlight, the fog that slowly lifts, leaving a champagne freshness in the air. I felt the *promise* of each new day, as well as the uncertainty of what that promise would produce.

The timing of activities in relation to the day is for me a compelling subject. I have got used to giving concerts at night, but when I was a child I hated to practise after the sun had set. It seemed to me then, and it still does, that the day is for accumulation, and that evening is for sharing: for the joy of playing, of using and expressing what you have stored during the day; for conversation, chamber music, relaxation.

The earliest part of the day should, I think, be devoted to stretching and

With Paul Tortelier at the Gstaad Festival in 1975.

exercising the body; the mind is not at its best until the body and circulation have been set in motion. If time allows, and especially if there are woods nearby, or fields or a beach or a hill, I like to go for an early-morning walk.

In the normal course of events, Millie, our devoted housekeeper, opens the mail; by 8.30 it is ready for me to deal with. I like to get as much done as possible early on – letters answered on my dictating machine, some telephone calls attended to – so that the rest of the day is relatively clear for music. Ever since I was a child, I have practised alone every morning.

However, I have occasionally given concerts in the morning. In Boston and in Washington DC, ladies' clubs used to invite an artist at a very good fee to give a short recital at eleven o'clock. I loved the feeling of having given my day's performance by noon.

I also like the Spanish and South American practice of beginning concerts at six o'clock. These, believe it or not, are called 'afternoon concerts', because an evening concert in these countries normally starts at ten or eleven. After a six o'clock concert, I can look forward to a long pleasant evening with friends. Even in England, where concerts begin at seven-thirty or eight, it is possible to sit down to a meal with friends by about ten o'clock.

I love, for some perverse reason, to rest when other people work. I find something especially luxurious in getting up very early, doing my exercises, practising for an hour or so, and then around eleven o'clock going to sleep! I do this on tour quite often, because late nights and travelling make the days so irregular. A morning nap sets me up for the rest of the day.

Touring makes life *far* removed from the ideal schedule. The fact that you can travel, sleep, practise, and give a concert, at any hour of the day, shows how adaptable the human body can be. Sleep comes easily to me: if I am tired, I can sleep anywhere and at any time.

The most important thing on tour is to eat well but never too much. Yesterday I had a meal, too large a one, at the Italian Embassy, and inevitably I was sleepy afterwards. Some ages-old law of cause and effect decrees that immediate gratifications always bring an element of regret.

This is not the case with music. When I play a piece well, it gives me joy not only for the rest of that day but for the rest of my life. Perhaps this is because the achievement has come from within myself, and is the result of my own efforts of thought and work.

A craftsman's satisfaction brings no subsequent regrets. Nor does eating, if it avoids excess fat, excess sugar, excess of any kind. Too often we are lured by momentary pleasures.

The Chinese have a very wholesome approach to food. They consider it important for food to give pleasure not only at the time of eating but even in its final elimination. The whole *trajectory* must be pleasurable! At all stages, Chinese food is simple and light.

In the west we have an unfortunate convention of serving a copious meal whenever we have guests. It is a rare host who can combine elegance and lightness in a meal. Michel Guérard does just this. His new style of cooking, *Cuisine Minceur*, is exquisite; during my sabbatical I had intended to make a pilgrimage to France so that I could meet him.

The Indians of the south have a similar skill, and use a special style of cooking for the holy men of the region. This kind of food and its preparation are considered conducive to prayer and meditation, to yoga exercises, the co-ordination of body and mind, and precision of movement. I once had such a meal served by my guru's family in Bombay. A whole range of delicate dishes were in preparation for two days. The result was the most wonderful gastronomic experience of my life. All was elegant, clean, and pure. A meal such as this leaves the mind clear, the stomach light, and mineral and vitamin requirements completely satisfied.

It was served and eaten with that innocent Indian gaiety, a carefree spirit that belongs to itself and is not the result of praise or triumph or success on the stock exchange. It is a spontaneous bubbling, like a fountain; nothing is forced.

What I most love about India is its all-inclusive conception of life: everything has meaning and purpose, from the most primitive to the most refined; everyone has his recognized, almost hallowed place – the warrior, the beggar, and the saint; good and evil are intertwined; creation and destruction are inseparable. No aspect of the mind, no function of the body, no rhythm or melodic twist, has escaped analysis by Indian scholars and sages down the centuries.

India is changing radically, with the new mobility of society spurred by education, science, and the types of work now required. The old order was no doubt ready for change, yet who can hope that the new will last?

RD: Who are the most evolved people you have ever met?

YM: I need time to think about that, but several names come immediately to mind, from a variety of professions: Enesco; Princess Irene of Greece; Harold Macmillan; Lord David Cecil; the American authoress, Willa Cather; Sidney

With Ravi Shankar and David Oistrakh in Paris before a concert to celebrate United Nations Day 1958.

Ehrman, a lawyer, who was so good to me and my family; George Prins, a diamond merchant, who used to be our neighbour here in Highgate; and Sir John Pilcher, former British Ambassador to Japan.

I would expect to find highly evolved people among the Sufis and Japanese Zen monks; and I am certain there are some extremely wise people among those who can scarcely read or write.

In India I met Homi Bhabha, first Chairman of their Atomic Energy Commission, a highly cultivated person, versed in the arts as well as in science. On a trip to New York a bright young reporter said to him: 'Mr Bhabha, how do you explain the fact that a famous scientist like yourself comes from such a primitive country?' He replied: 'You are quite right. We didn't invent the motor car or the aeroplane. We are not a great industrial nation. But you must bear in mind that for thousands of years we have had hot dry summers, and when we don't feel like doing any more work we just sit under the shade of a tree and *think!*'

RD: I often hear artistic people speak of the need to preserve and nurture their own particular gifts. Some speak of this as being their prime responsibility in life.

YM: Whatever we have, we have been given *on lease*. I don't own the use of my body. I certainly don't own my wife or my children. I don't even feel that I own my house. Like the Red Indians, I believe that land is to be used in the same way as air and water and all that the earth yields – with respect and gratitude, and always mindful of the needs of future generations.

RD: Did your parents foster a conception of your musical ability being on lease?

YM: My sisters and I learned this from them indirectly, by their example and selflessness.

It is my responsibility not only to preserve my violin technique for as long as possible, but also to ensure that it continues to evolve, and becomes both more precise and more fluid, and more responsive to my expressive aims.

Every day I work to perfect my technique. I can never own it. If I were to stop practising for a month it would take another month, or even longer, to make up for time lost.

Like a bondsman who is working to gain his freedom, I am also under an obligation to my body. I do exercises every day and enjoy doing them, just as I enjoy my violin practice. Everything in life which is of value requires continuous effort and renewal.

RD: Apart from the help you have gained in your violin playing – in greater flexibility and control – how great a contribution does yoga make to your life?

YM: The meditative quality of the eastern is remarkable: the ability to think pointedly and concentratedly about a given subject, or clearing the mind and not thinking about anything at all, just letting things be. Centuries ago, by concentration and contemplation, yogis discovered truths about the functioning of the body which are now being verified by modern medical science. The way of the West is analysis, dissection, measurement; the way of the yogi is pure awareness of what is going on within.

Unfortunately I don't give as much time to the practice as I should, but yoga does make a great contribution. It enables me to regulate my breathing, quieten my mind, and do certain exercises in stretching. Also I have been made *aware* of certain subconscious processes, of posture and balance, of the co-ordination of joints, and the use of the body to its fullest potential.

Yoga, if practised with reverence, is a way of looking after the body we have been entrusted with, keeping the inner and outer self clean, the reflexes alert, the lungs flexible. The glory of yoga is that it can lead to expansion of every kind – physical, mental, spiritual.

Deep breathing, and the extra intake of oxygen, gives full freedom of motion to the joints, but that is only one of the benefits. You cannot breathe quietly if you have any sense of guilt, anxiety, envy, or impatience. The feedback from this is an enhanced ability to control unworthy emotions and motives during the course of the day.

I do lose my temper occasionally – not necessarily at the most appropriate moments. One of the troubles with losing your temper is that you lose it at moments when you don't choose to! I admire people, like my mother, who can deliberately lose – or, rather, show – their temper to create a desired effect. With my mother, it was a controlled emotion designed to get the children to do their best: it was short-lived, never more than necessary, and carefully graded to the requirements of the occasion. I am not at all like that; for one thing, I have no acting capacity at all, and this is probably one of the bases of my efforts at achieving honesty. I have absolutely no gift for subterfuge!

My wife has a fund of wonderful quotations. From time to time she will look over a speech I will soon be giving, and suggest one or two apt quotations to insert. Afterwards, she invariably says: 'I will *never* suggest any more quotations. Your integrity is such that you can't read them with conviction, simply because someone else has found them for you.'

Sometimes, as with a long and deeply moving quotation, I am able to read with full conviction. In the middle of a lecture I gave recently entitled *Happiness*, I quoted from a letter of 1855 by Chief Seathl, a Red Indian, to President Franklin Pierce. What he wrote is so relevant to our time – to *all* time – that I should very much like to read you the text:

> There is no quiet place in the white man's cities. No place to hear the leaves of autumn or the rustle of insects' wings. Perhaps because I am a savage and do not understand, the clatter insults the ears. And what is life if a man cannot hear the lovely call of the whippoorwill, or the argument of frogs around a pond at night? The Indian prefers the soft sound of the wind darting over the face of the pond; and the smell of the wind itself, cleansed by a mid-day rain or scented with pine. The air is precious to the red man, because all share the same breath – the beasts, the trees, and man himself. The white man does not seem to notice the air he breathes. Like a man dying for many days, he is numb to the smell of his own stench.
>
> If I decide to accept [here Chief Seathl refers to land which the white man would like to buy], I will make one condition: the white man must treat the beasts of this land as his own brothers. I am a savage and do not understand any other way. I have seen a thousand rotting buffaloes on the prairies, left by the white man who shot them from a passing train. I am a savage and do not understand how the smoking iron horse can be more important than the buffalo that we kill only to live. What is man without the beasts? If all the beasts were gone, man would die from great loneliness of spirit, for whatever happens to the beast also happens to man. All things are connected. Whatever befalls the earth befalls the sons of the earth.
>
> Our children have seen their fathers humbled in defeat. Our warriors have felt shame. After defeat they spend their days in idleness, and contaminate their bodies with sweet food and strong drink. It matters little where we pass the rest of our days – they are not many. A few more hours, a few more winters, and none of the children of the great tribes that once lived on this earth, or that roamed in small bands in the woods, will be left to mourn the graves of people once as powerful and hopeful as yours.

Opposite: Menuhin demonstrates one kind of 'balance' to conductor Rudolph Barshai and colleagues.

One thing we know, and the white man may one day discover the truth of it: our God is the same as your God. You may now think that you own Him in the same way that you wish to own our land. But you cannot. He is the God of man. And His compassion is equal for the red man and the white. This earth is precious to Him, and to harm the earth is to heap contempt upon its creator.

The whites too shall pass – perhaps sooner than other tribes. Continue to contaminate your bed and you will one night suffocate in your own waste. When the buffalo are all slaughtered, the wild horses all tamed, the secret corners of the forest heavy with the scent of many men, and the view of the ripe hills blotted by talking wives, where is the thicket? Gone. Where is the eagle? Gone. This marks the end of living and the beginning of survival.

We might understand if we knew what the white man dreams, what hopes he describes to his children on long winter nights, what visions he burns into their minds so that they will wish for tomorrow. But we are savages. The white man's dreams are hidden from us. And because they are hidden, we will go our own way.

If we agree to sell our land, it will be to secure the Indian reservation you have promised us. There, perhaps, we may live out our brief days as we wish.

When the last red man has vanished from the earth, and the memory of him is like the shadow of a cloud moving across the prairie, these shores and forests will still hold the spirits of my people, for we love the earth as the newborn loves his mother's heartbeat.

INDEX

INDEX

INDEX